Cambridge Elements ≡

Elements in the Philosophy of Immanuel Kant
edited by
Desmond Hogan
Princeton University
Howard Williams
University of Cardiff
Allen Wood
Indiana University

T0286912

INTRODUCING KANT'S *CRITIQUE OF PURE REASON*

Paul Guyer
Brown University
Allen Wood
Indiana University

CAMBRIDGE
UNIVERSITY PRESS

CAMBRIDGE
UNIVERSITY PRESS

University Printing House, Cambridge CB2 8BS, United Kingdom

One Liberty Plaza, 20th Floor, New York, NY 10006, USA

477 Williamstown Road, Port Melbourne, VIC 3207, Australia

314–321, 3rd Floor, Plot 3, Splendor Forum, Jasola District Centre,
New Delhi – 110025, India

79 Anson Road, #06–04/06, Singapore 079906

Cambridge University Press is part of the University of Cambridge.

It furthers the University's mission by disseminating knowledge in the pursuit of
education, learning, and research at the highest international levels of excellence.

www.cambridge.org
Information on this title: www.cambridge.org/9781108795296
DOI: 10.1017/9781108894869

First published 2021

A catalogue record for this publication is available from the British Library.

ISBN 978-1-108-79529-6 Paperback
ISSN 2397-9461 (online)
ISSN 2514-3824 (print)

Introducing Kant's *Critique of Pure Reason*

Elements in the Philosophy of Immanuel Kant

DOI: 10.1017/9781108894869
First published online: March 2021

Paul Guyer
Brown University
Allen Wood
Indiana University

Author for correspondence: Paul Guyer, Paul_Guyer@brown.edu

Abstract: This Element surveys the place of the *Critique of Pure Reason* in Kant's overall philosophical project and describes and analyzes the main arguments of the work. It also surveys the developments in Kant's thought that led to the first critique, and provides an account of the genesis of the book during the "silent decade" of its composition in the 1770s based on Kant's handwritten notes from the period.

Keywords: Kant, transcendental idealism, causation, free will, God

ISBNs: 9781108795296 (PB), 9781108894869 (OC)
ISSNs: 2397-9461 (online), 2514-3824 (print)

Contents

Immanuel Kant's *Critique of Pure Reason* is one of the seminal and monumental works in the history of Western philosophy.[1] Published in May 1781, when its author was already fifty-seven years old, and substantially revised for its second edition six years later, the book was both the culmination of three decades of its author's often very private work and the starting point for nearly two more decades of his rapidly evolving but now very public philosophical thought. In the more than two centuries since the book was first published, it has been the constant object of scholarly interpretation and a continuous source of inspiration to inventive philosophers. To tell the whole story of the book's influence would be to write the history of philosophy since Kant, and that is beyond our intention here. After a summary of the *Critique*'s structure and argument, this introduction will sketch its genesis and evolution from Kant's earliest metaphysical treatise in 1755 to the publication of the first edition of the *Critique* in 1781 and its revision for the second edition of 1787.

1 The Argument of the *Critique*

The strategy of the *Critique*.   In the conclusion to his second critique, the *Critique of Practical Reason* (CPrR) of 1788, Kant famously wrote, "Two things fill the mind with ever new and increasing admiration and awe the more often and more enduringly reflection is occupied with them: **the starry heavens above me and the moral law within me**" (CPrR 5: 161). This motto could just as well have served for virtually all of Kant's philosophical works, and certainly for the *Critique of Pure Reason*. From the outset of his career, Kant had been concerned to establish the basic principles of scientific knowledge of the world, thereby explaining our knowledge of the "starry heavens." Almost as early in his career, Kant was intent on showing that human freedom, understood not only as the presupposition of morality but also as the ultimate value served and advanced by the moral law, is compatible with the truth of modern science. The first *Critique* is complex, however, because Kant argues on several fronts. Like Descartes, Locke, and Hume, Kant felt he had to rein in the pretensions of traditional metaphysics, which was represented for him by the school of Christian Wolff (1679–1754) and his followers, especially Alexander Gottlieb Baumgarten (1714–62). Their position, which Kant called "dogmatism," was compared in the preface to the

---

1. This text is an abridged and updated version of the Editor's Introduction to our translation of the *Critique of Pure Reason*, published by Cambridge University Press in 1998. All citations to that edition are by the first ("A") and second ("B") edition pagination of Kant's original text, reproduced in our translation. All other works of Kant are quoted from the volumes of the Cambridge edition listed at the end of this work, and passages are located by the volume and page number of the *Akademie* edition, also listed at the end, which are reproduced in the margins of all volumes of the Cambridge edition.

Critique to the despotic ministry of an absolute monarchy. Kant held dogmatism to be capricious, opinionated, faction-ridden and consequently unstable and open to the contempt of rational observers.

Yet Kant wanted to distinguish his own *critical* stance toward dogmatism from several other ways of rejecting it, which he regarded as equally dangerous. The first of these is *skepticism*, the position Kant took David Hume (1711–76) to advocate. Another was the "way of ideas" described in John Locke's (1632–1704) *Essay Concerning Human Understanding* (1690), which grounded knowledge solely on ideas acquired in the course of individual experience. Yet another philosophical stance was what Kant called *indifferentism*; it did not reject metaphysical assertions themselves, but scorned the attempt to argue for them systematically and rigorously. Here he had in mind a number of popular philosophers who agreed with dogmatists on metaphysical issues such as the existence of God and the immortality of the soul, but were unconvinced by the scholastic subtlety of their propositions and proofs. They held that the metaphysical beliefs we need are given simply through "healthy understanding" or common sense.

While Kant attempted to criticize and limit the scope of traditional rationalist metaphysics, he also sought to defend against the possibility of *a priori* knowledge, knowledge originating independently of experience, against the empiricist point that no particular experience (or *a posteriori* knowledge) could justify claims to universal and necessary validity. Just as Kant compared dogmatic metaphysicians to defenders of despotism, so he likened skeptics to nomads who abhor any form of permanent civil society and Lockeans to calumniators who would foist a false and degrading genealogy on the monarch. Those who would pretend indifference to metaphysical inquiries he charged with being closet dogmatists, like supporters of a corrupt regime who scoff at its defects and feign ironic detachment from it but have no independent convictions of their own.

Kant's position thus required him not only to undermine the arguments of traditional metaphysics but also to put in their place a scientific metaphysics, limited to what is required for ordinary experience and its extension by natural science. Thus Kant had to fight a war on several different fronts, in which he had to establish against both dogmatists and empiricists that many metaphysical questions are unanswerable; but he had to defend against both empiricists and skeptics parts of the very positions he was attacking, such as the possibility of *a priori* cognition of the fundamental principles required for natural science. And although he wanted to prove to the indifferentists that a science of metaphysics is important, he also wanted to embrace part of their position as well. For in regard to some insoluble metaphysical questions, Kant thought that we must defend a kind of commonsense belief in God, freedom, and immortality because morality has a vital stake in them.

The structure of the *Critique*.   This complex program helps explain the enormous complexity of the structure and argument of the *Critique of Pure Reason*. To many readers, the "architectonic" of the *Critique* has been a barrier to understanding it, but a brief overview of the main divisions can illuminate its contents. Despite the profound originality of its contents, Kant actually borrowed much of the book's structure from well-known models. After the preface (which was completely rewritten for the second edition) and the introduction, the *Critique* is divided into two main parts, the "Doctrine of Elements" and the "Doctrine of Method." Such a distinction was common in German logic textbooks; in Kant's hands, it becomes a distinction between his fundamental exposition of *a priori* cognition and its limits, in the "Doctrine of Elements," and subsequent reflections on its methodological implications. The "Doctrine of Method" provides contrasts between mathematical and philosophical proof and between theoretical and practical reasoning, as well as contrasts between his own critical method and dogmatic, empirical, and skeptical methods of philosophy.

  The "Doctrine of Elements" is divided into two main (although very disproportionately sized) parts: the "Transcendental Aesthetic" and the "Transcendental Logic." The former considers the *a priori* contributions of the fundamental forms of our *sensibility*, namely space and time, to our knowledge; the latter considers the *a priori* contributions, both genuine and spurious, to our knowledge made by the human intellect. This division is derived from Baumgarten, who introduced "aesthetics" as the title for the science of "lower" or "sensitive cognition" in contrast to "logic" as the science of "higher" or conceptual cognition.[2] At the time he wrote the *Critique*, however, Kant rejected Baumgarten's supposition that there could be a *science of taste* (what we now call "aesthetics"), and instead appropriated the term for his theory of the contribution of the forms of sensibility to knowledge in general (A21/B35–6). After briefly distinguishing between "general logic" and "transcendental logic" – the former being the basic science of the forms of thought regardless of its object and the latter the science of the basic forms for the thought of objects (A50–7/ B74–82) – Kant then splits the "Transcendental Logic" into two main divisions, the "Transcendental Analytic" and the "Transcendental Dialectic." This distinction derives from a sixteenth-century Aristotelian distinction between the logic of truth and the logic of probability, a distinction employed in eighteenth-century Germany by the Jena professor Joachim Georg Darjes (1714–92). Kant uses it instead to distinguish between the positive

2. See Baumgarten's *Meditationes philosophicae* (1735), §§115–16, *Metaphysica* (1739), §533, and *Aesthetica* (1750–58), §1.

contributions of the understanding, working in cooperation with sensibility (as described in the "Transcendental Analytic"), and the false and deceptive attempts of reason working independently of sensibility to provide metaphysical insight into objects beyond possible experience (the "Transcendental Dialectic"). The "Transcendental Analytic" is then further divided into two books: the "Analytic of Concepts" and the "Analytic of Principles." The former argues for the universal and necessary validity of the pure concepts of the understanding, or the *categories*, such as the concepts of substance and causation; the latter argues for the validity of fundamental principles of empirical *judgment* employing those categories, such as the principles of the conservation of substance and the universality of causation.

The "Transcendental Dialectic" is also divided into two books, "On the Concepts of Pure Reason" and "On the Dialectical Inferences of Pure Reason." In the first, Kant explains how pure reason generates ideas of metaphysical entities such as the soul, the world as a whole, and God; the second explores critically the attempts to prove the reality of those ideas by extending beyond their proper limits the patterns of inference which are valid only within the limits of human sensibility. The division of the "Transcendental Analytic" into the "Analytic of Concepts" and "Analytic of Principles," then followed by the "Dialectical Inferences of Pure Reason," replicates the traditional division of logic textbooks into three sections on *concepts*, *judgments*, and *inferences*. Kant uses this structure to argue that the *concepts* of pure understanding, when applied to the forms of *sensibility*, give rise to sound principles of *judgment*, but that inferences of pure reason performed without respect to the limits of sensibility give rise only to metaphysical illusion. The treatment of dialectical inferences is in turn divided into three sections, "The Paralogisms of Pure Reason," "The Antinomy of Pure Reason," and "The Ideal of Pure Reason." In each section Kant exposes metaphysically fallacious arguments about, respectively, the nature of the soul, the world as a totality, and the existence of God. These divisions are also derived from Kant's predecessors: Wolff and Baumgarten divided metaphysics into "general metaphysics," or "ontology," and "special metaphysics," in turn divided into "rational psychology," "rational cosmology," and "rational theology." Kant replaces their "ontology" with the constructive doctrine of his own "Transcendental Analytic" (see A247/B303), and then presents his criticism of dogmatic metaphysics based on pure reason alone by demolishing the special metaphysics of rational psychology, cosmology, and theology.

Kant divides the "Doctrine of Method" into four chapters, the "Discipline," the "Canon," the "Architectonic," and the "History of Pure Reason." The first two of these sections are much more detailed than the last two. In the "Discipline of Pure Reason," Kant provides an extended contrast between the nature of mathematical proof and that of philosophical argument, and offers important commentary on his own "critical" or "transcendental" method. In the "Canon of Pure Reason," he prepares the way for his subsequent moral philosophy, contrasting the method of theoretical philosophy to that of practical philosophy. He also gives the first outline of the argument that runs through all three critiques, namely that although *theoretical reason* can never yield *knowledge* of God, freedom, and immortality, *practical reason* can justify rational *belief or faith* in such things. The last two parts of the "Doctrine of Method," the "Architectonic of Pure Reason" and the "History of Pure Reason," recapitulate the contrasts between Kant's own critical philosophical method and those of the dogmatists, empiricists, and skeptics with which he began, treating these contrasts in both systematic and historical terms. In the few pages of his "History of Pure Reason" Kant outlines the history of modern philosophy in terms of the distinction between rationalism and empiricism that we still use, while representing his own critical philosophy as the transcendence of both.

Within the organization of the *Critique of Pure Reason* as just presented, we now provide a brief résumé of its contents.

"Introduction": the idea of transcendental philosophy. Although Kant himself often suggests that the negative side of his project, the critique of dogmatic metaphysics, is the most important, the *Critique*'s greatest influence has been exercised by Kant's positive doctrine of the *a priori* elements of human knowledge. In the introduction, Kant argues that our mathematical, physical, and everyday knowledge of nature requires certain judgments that are "synthetic" rather than "analytic"; that is, they go beyond what can be known solely in virtue of the contents of the concepts involved in them – and yet these judgments are also knowable *a priori*, that is, independently of any particular experience. He entitles the question of how synthetic *a priori* judgments are possible the "general problem of pure reason" (B19), and proposes an entirely new science in order to answer it (A10–16/B24–30).

This new science Kant calls "transcendental" (A11/B25). It does not deal directly with objects of empirical cognition, but investigates the conditions of the possibility of our experience of them by examining the mental capacities that are required even for the possibility of any cognition of objects. Kant agrees with Locke that we have no innate knowledge, that is, no knowledge of any particular propositions implanted in us by God or nature prior to the commencement of our individual experience. Experience, however, is the product both of external objects affecting our sensibility and of the operation of our cognitive faculties in response to this effect (A1, B1). Kant's claim is that we can have "pure" or *a priori* cognition of the contributions to experience that are made by

6 Philosophy of Immanuel Kant

the operation of these faculties themselves rather than by the effect of external objects on us. Kant divides our cognitive capacities into *sensibility*: our receptivity to the effects of external objects acting on us, through which these objects are given to us in empirical intuition, and *understanding*: our active faculty for relating the data of intuition by thinking them under concepts and forming judgments about them (A19/B33).

"Transcendental Aesthetic": space and time; transcendental idealism. Despite its brevity, the "Transcendental Aesthetic" argues for a series of striking, paradoxical, and even revolutionary theses that determine the course of the whole remainder of the *Critique* and that have been the subject of a large proportion of the scholarly interpretation and controversy devoted to the *Critique* over the last two centuries. Kant attempts to distinguish the contribution to cognition made by our receptive faculty of sensibility from that made solely by the objects that affect us (A21–2/B36). He argues that space and time are pure forms of all intuition contributed by our own faculty of sensibility, and therefore that we can have *a priori* knowledge regarding them. Here Kant also attempts to resolve the debate about space and time between the Newtonians, who held space and time to be self-subsisting entities existing independently of the objects that occupy them, and the Leibnizians, who held space and time to be systems of relations, conceptual constructs based on nonrelational properties inhering in spatiotemporally related things.[3] Kant's new alternative is that space and time are neither subsistent beings nor inherent in things as they are in themselves, but are rather only forms of our sensibility. Only in this way, Kant argues, can we adequately account for our knowledge of the geometrical and mathematical properties of space and time as singular but infinite magnitudes. Kant hereby rejects Leibniz's account of space and time as mere relations abstracted from antecedently existing objects and accepts a Newtonian conception of absolute space and time, but only as the structure of human representation, not of the divine representation of reality (A22–5/B37–41, A30–2/B46–9).

Kant's thesis that space and time are pure forms of intuition leads him to the paradoxical conclusion that although space and time are *empirically real*, they are *transcendentally ideal*, and so are the objects given in them. Although the precise meaning of this claim remains subject to debate, in general terms it is the claim that it is only from the human standpoint that we can speak of space, time, and the spatiotemporality of the objects of experience, from which Kant inferred that we cognize these things not as they are in themselves but only as they appear under the conditions of our sensibility (A26–30/B42–5, A32–48/

---

3. The correspondence between Leibniz and Newton's spokesman Samuel Clarke was published in 1717, and in German in 1720.

B49–73). This is Kant's *transcendental idealism*, which is employed throughout his critical philosophy in a variety of ways, both positively and negatively, and has been interpreted, attacked, and defended in a wide variety of ways over more than two centuries.

"Transcendental Analytic": the metaphysical and transcendental deductions. In the first part of the "Transcendental Analytic," the "Analytic of Concepts," Kant presents the understanding as the source of certain concepts that are *a priori* and are conditions of the possibility of experience. These twelve basic concepts, which Kant calls the *categories*, are *fundamental concepts of an object in general* or the fundamental general concepts of objects, that is, the forms for any particular concepts of objects, and in conjunction with the *a priori* forms of intuition are the basis of all synthetic *a priori* cognition. In an initial section of the "Transcendental Analytic" (A66–81/B91–116), which in the second edition of the *Critique* Kant named the "metaphysical deduction" (B159), Kant derives the twelve categories from a table of the twelve *logical functions* or forms of judgments, the logically significant aspects of all judgments. Kant's idea is that just as there are certain essential features of all judgments, so there must be certain corresponding ways in which we form the concepts of objects so that judgments may be about those objects. There are four main logically significant aspects of judgments: their *quantity*, or the scope of their subject-terms; their *quality*, which concerns whether and how the predicate-term is affirmed or denied; their *relation*, or whether they assert a relation just between a subject and a predicate or between two or more subject-predicate judgments; and their *modality*, whether they assert a possible, actual, or necessary truth. Under each of these four headings there are supposed to be three different options: A judgment may be universal, particular, or singular; affirmative, negative, or infinite; categorical, hypothetical, or disjunctive; and problematic, assertoric, or apodictic, that is, possibly, actually, or necessarily true. Corresponding to these twelve logical possibilities, Kant posits twelve fundamental categories for conceiving of the quantity, quality, relation, and modality of objects (A70/B95, A80/B106). Kant's claims about the logical functions of judgment and the twelve corresponding categories have remained controversial ever since Kant first made them.

Kant's even more ambitious claim is that these concepts apply universally and necessarily to the intuitions that are given in our experience, so that in some sense all of our experience (even of ourselves) is objective, that is, is subject to concepts that function as rules for the determinate relation of representations in experience (B137). (It must be kept in mind that for Kant "object" does not necessarily mean *external* object; rather, it will be key to Kant's whole argument that inner sense or internal experience is also part of the rule-governed world and in that sense objective). Kant argues for this thesis in the "Transcendental Deduction of the Categories," the chapter which he says in the first edition of the *Critique* cost him the most labor (Axvi), but which he then rewrote almost in its entirety for the second edition (A84–130/B116–69). In both versions of the *Critique*, Kant's argument rests on the premise that any and all of our experiences can be ascribed to a single identical subject, through a mental act he calls the "transcendental unity of apperception." Experience is possible only if the elements given in intuition are synthetically combined through this activity so as to present us with objects that are thought through the categories. The categories are therefore held to apply to objects not because the objects make the categories possible, but rather because combination according to the categories makes possible the representation of objects of experience. We do not abstract the categories from the experience of objects, but constitute the experience of objects by the use of the categories.

Principles of pure understanding.   Even if the transcendental deduction succeeds in establishing that the categories do apply to all possible data for experience, it does so only abstractly and collectively. That is, it does not specify how each category applies necessarily to the objects given in experience, nor does it show that all of the categories must be applied to objects. To establish these further claims is Kant's task in book II of the "Transcendental Analytic," the "Analytic of Principles." This book is in turn divided into three chapters, "The Schematism of the Pure Concepts of the Understanding," the "System of All Principles of Pure Understanding," and "On the Ground of the Distinction of All Objects in General into Phenomena and Noumena." In the first of these chapters, Kant shows how the logical content of the categories derived from the metaphysical deduction is to be transformed into a content applicable to the data of our senses. In the second, he demonstrates principles of judgment showing that all of the categories must be applied to our experience by means of arguments that some interpreters have thought sufficient to prove the objective validity of the categories independently of the prior transcendental deduction. In the third chapter Kant argues that because the categories have a determinate use only when applied to spatiotemporal data, they also have a determinate cognitive use only when applied to appearances ("phenomena"). By means of the categories things as they are in themselves ("noumena") might be *thought* but they cannot be *known*.

In the "Schematism," Kant argues that the categories, whose content has thus far been derived solely from the logical structure of judgments, must be made applicable to objects whose form has thus far been specified solely by the pure forms of space and time. He argues that this can be done by associating each category with a "transcendental schema," a form or relation in intuition that is an appropriate representation of the corresponding logical form or relation. In particular, Kant argues that each category must be associated with a *temporal* schema. For example, the schema of the logical conception of ground and consequence is the concept of *causality* as rule-governed temporal succession: The concept of a cause is that of "the real upon which, whenever it is posited, something else always follows," or "the succession of the manifold insofar as it is subject to a rule" (A144/B183). The subsequent chapter on the "Principles" will show that although the content of the transcendental schemata for the categories may be explicated in purely temporal terms, the *use* of these schemata in turn depends upon judgments about the *spatial* properties and relations of at least some objects of empirical judgment. The principles expressing the universal and necessary application of the categories to objects given in space and time are precisely the synthetic *a priori* judgments that are to be demonstrated by Kant's critical replacement for traditional metaphysics.

In the second chapter of the "Analytic of Principles," the "System of All Principles of Pure Understanding," Kant organizes the principles of pure understanding under four headings corresponding to the four groups of categories. For each of the first two groups of categories, those listed under "Quantity" and "Quality," Kant supplies a single "mathematical" principle meant to guarantee the applicability to empirical objects of certain parts of mathematics, which are in turn supposed to be associated with certain parts of the logic of judgment. The first principle, under the title "Axioms of Intuition," guarantees that the *a priori* mathematics of extensive magnitudes, where wholes are measured by their discrete parts, applies to empirical objects because these are given in space and time which are themselves extensive magnitudes (A162–6/B202–7). The general implication of this argument is that the empirical use of the logical quantifiers (one, some, all) depends on the division of the empirical manifold into distinct spatiotemporal regions. The second principle, under the title of the "Anticipations of Perception," guarantees that the mathematics of *intensive* magnitudes applies to the "real in space," or that properties such as color or heat, or material forces such as weight or impenetrability, must exist in a continuum of degrees because our sensations of them are continuously variable (A166–76/B207–18). Here Kant's argument is that since the use of the logical functions of affirmation and negation is dependent on the presence or absence of sensations that come in continuously varying degrees, the empirical use of the categories of "Quality" is connected with the mathematics of intensive magnitudes in a way that could not have been predicted from an analysis of the logical content of these categories themselves.

Switching from "mathematical" to "dynamical" principles, the third section of the "System," the "Analogies of Experience," concerns the necessary *relations* among what is given in space and time, and thus gives expression to the necessary conditions for the application of the categories of "Relation" to empirical objects. In the first Analogy, Kant argues that the unity of time implies that all change must consist in the alteration of states in an underlying substance, whose existence and quantity must be unchangeable or conserved (A182–6/B224–32). In the second Analogy, Kant argues that we can make determinate judgments about the objective succession of events as contrasted to merely subjective successions of representations only if every objective alteration follows a necessary rule of succession, or a causal law (A186–211/B232–56). In the third Analogy, Kant argues that determinate judgments that objects (more precisely, states of substance) in different regions of space exist simultaneously are possible only if such objects stand in the mutual causal relation of community or reciprocal interaction (A211–15/B256–62). Many interpreters consider the chapter on the Analogies of Experience the most important section of the *Critique* because it is supposed to supply the answer to Hume's skeptical doubt about causality, while the third Analogy is the basis of Kant's rejection of Leibniz's denial of real interaction between substances. Both what the second Analogy is intended to prove and how the proof is supposed to proceed have been disputed almost as intensely as the philosophical question as to whether Kant's reply to Hume is successful. In the first edition of the *Critique*, the final section of the "System of Principles," the "Postulates of Empirical Thought," provides conditions for the empirical use of the modal categories of possibility, existence, and necessity, and argues that our justified theoretical use of the categories of both *possibility* and *necessity* is in fact confined to the sphere of the *actual*, that is, that which is actually given in experience (A218–35/B265–74, 279—87). In the second edition, however, Kant inserted a new argument, the "Refutation of Idealism" (B274–9), which attempts to show that the very possibility of our consciousness of ourselves presupposes the existence of an external world of objects that are not only represented as spatially outside us but are also conceived to exist independently of our subjective representations of them. Although the implications of this argument have been intensely debated, it seems to confirm Kant's claim in the *Prolegomena to Any Future Metaphysics* (4:288–94) that his "transcendental idealism" is a "critical" or "formal" idealism, which unlike traditional idealism does not deny the *real existence* of the objects distinct from ourselves that are represented as being in space and time.

In the third chapter of the "Analytic of Principles," on phenomena and noumena, Kant emphasizes that because the categories must always be applied to data provided by sensibility in order to provide cognition, they give us knowledge only of things as they appear ("phenomena"). Through pure understanding (*nous* in Greek) we may *think* of objects independently of their being given in sensibility, but we can never *cognize* them as such nonsensible entities ("noumena") (A235–60/B294–315). For this reason, Kant says it is legitimate for us to speak of noumena only "in a negative sense," meaning things as they may be in themselves independently of our representation of them, but not noumena "in a positive sense," which would be things known through a pure understanding alone.

At this point in the *Critique* Kant has completed his argument that synthetic *a priori* principles of theoretical cognition are the necessary conditions of the application of the categories to sensible data structured by the pure forms of intuition. The next part of his project is the critical demonstration that traditional metaphysics consists largely of illusions arising from the attempt to acquire knowledge of all things (the soul, the world as a whole, and God) as they are in themselves by the use of reason alone regardless of the limits of sensibility. The bulk of this argument is reserved for the "Transcendental Dialectic," but Kant makes a start on it with the interesting appendix that completes the "Transcendental Analytic" entitled the "Amphiboly of Concepts of Reflection" (A160–92/B316–49). In this appendix Kant presents his criticism of Leibniz's monadology. He argues that through a confusion (or "amphiboly") Leibniz has taken mere features of concepts through which we think things, specifically concepts of comparison or reflection such as "same" and "different" or "inner" and "outer," which are in fact never applied directly to things but only applied to them through more determinate concepts, as if they were features of the objects themselves. Kant thereby rejects the Leibnizian-Wolffian account of such metaphysical concepts as essence, identity, and possibility, and reinforces his own insistence that empirical judgments of real possibility require sensible conditions in addition to logical intelligibility and noncontradictoriness.

The "Transcendental Dialectic": the critique of metaphysics. The second division of the "Transcendental Logic" turns to the main destructive task of the *Critique of Pure Reason*, and that which gives the book its name: the task of displaying the *limits* of metaphysics. But Kant's aim in the "Dialectic" is not only the negative one of demonstrating the failure of a metaphysics that transcends the boundaries of possible experience. He also has the positive aim of demonstrating that the questions that preoccupy metaphysics are inevitable, and that the arguments of metaphysics, although deceptive, should not be dismissed without sympathetic comprehension. Kant argues that they tempt us for genuine reasons, inherent in the nature of human reason itself, and when these grounds are properly understood they can be put to good use for the causes of both human knowledge and human morality. This argument is the basis for Kant's theory of the regulative use of the ideas of reason in scientific inquiry, which Kant first suggests in the Appendix to the "Transcendental Dialectic" and then later elaborates in the *Critique of the Power of Judgment.*

The Leibnizian-Wolffian tradition was represented in Alexander Gottlieb Baumgarten's *Metaphysica* (1739). Kant used this as the textbook for his lectures on metaphysics for virtually his entire career. Like other textbooks on the Wolffian pattern, *Metaphysica* was divided into four parts: ontology, psychology, cosmology, and theology. The "Transcendental Aesthetic" and "Analytic" are Kant's critical replacement for Wolffian ontology. The "Transcendental Dialectic," however, is dedicated to arguing that the other three parts of the rationalist system are pseudosciences founded on inevitable illusions of human reason when it extends itself beyond the limits of sensibility. Kant does not present the three rationalistic pseudosciences as mere historical curiosities, but interprets them as inevitable products of human reason by deriving them from the unconditioned use of the three traditional forms of syllogism: categorical, hypothetical, and disjunctive. Seeking the unconditioned subject to which all our thoughts relate as predicates, we generate the idea of the soul as a simple, nonempirical substance; seeking the unconditioned in respect of any of several hypothetical series arising in the world (of composition or extension, of decomposition or division, of cause and effect) leads to ideas such as that of a first event in time, an outer limit to space, a simple substance and a first cause. Finally, Kant derives the idea of a most real being or God as the ideal ground of the real properties constituting all other things.

The opening book of the "Transcendental Dialectic" is therefore a derivation and even a limited defense of the *transcendental ideas* of the immortal soul, free will, and God, with which dogmatic metaphysics has always been preoccupied (A293–338/B349–96). *Reason*, traditionally thought to be the highest of our cognitive faculties, has a "logical use" in which it simply draws inferences from principles, but also a "real use" in which it seeks to base series of ordinary inferences, such as those from cause to effect, in ultimate foundational principles, such as the idea of an uncaused first cause. The ideas of such ultimate principles are generated *a priori* by the faculty of reason when it seeks, through regressive syllogistic reasoning, for what is unconditioned in respect of the objects given in experience, according to the principles of understanding that govern these objects. In particular, it is the three categories of *relation* when used without regard to the limits of sensibility that give rise to the chief ideas of metaphysics: The concept of substance gives rise to the idea of the soul as the ultimate subject, the concept of causation gives rise to the idea of the world-whole as a completed series of conditions, and the concept of community gives rise to the idea of God as the common ground of all possibilities. Kant suggests that each of the three relational categories gives rise to a distinctive form of syllogistic inference. We form the idea of the series of such inferences as being terminated in an unconditioned ground, but the purely rational idea of anything unconditioned cannot yield theoretical knowledge of an unconditioned subject, series, and set of all possibilities. Yet since sensibility is always conditioned (e.g., any space is always surrounded by more space), there could be no theoretical confirmation of the existence of the unconditioned even if sensibility were involved.

The second and by far the larger book of the "Dialectic" expounds "The Dialectical Inferences of Pure Reason" in great detail. The errors of rational psychology are diagnosed under the rubric of "The Paralogisms of Pure Reason," those of rational cosmology under the rubric of "The Antinomy of Pure Reason," and those of rational theology under the rubric of "The Ideal of Pure Reason."

The "Paralogisms."   Rational psychology is the topic of the "Paralogisms" (or fallacious syllogistic inferences) of pure reason, which argue invalidly from the formal unity, simplicity, and identity of the *thought* of the subject of thinking or the "I" to the conclusion that the *soul* is a real and simple (hence indestructible) substance that is self-identical throughout all experience (A341–66). In the first edition, the "Paralogisms" included a fourth part, which defends the reality of external appearance in space simply by reducing objects in space to one form of immediate representation (A366–405). This response to idealism was replaced in the second edition with the "Refutation of Idealism," which (as we saw) argues for the real existence of objects in space and time although for the transcendental ideality of their spatial and temporal form. In the second edition, the entire chapter on the paralogisms was rewritten and simplified (B406–22); to fill the place of the superseded fourth paralogism, Kant adds an argument that his dualism of appearance and reality undercuts the traditional dualism of mind and body.

The "Antinomies."   The longest and most painstaking part of the "Transcendental Dialectic" is the "Antinomy of Pure Reason," which deals with the topics of rational cosmology (A405–583/B432–611); indeed, Kant originally thought that all of the errors of metaphysics could be diagnosed in the form of these antinomies. Here Kant argues that reason's natural illusions are not merely revealed by subtle philosophical analysis but unavoidably manifest themselves in the form of outright contradictions, each side of which seems naturally plausible. Kant argues that unless we accept the transcendental idealist distinction between appearances and things in themselves, we will be committed to accepting mutually incompatible arguments, arguments both that there must be a first beginning of the world in time and that there cannot be, that there must be limits to the world in space and that there cannot be (the two halves of the first antinomy), both that there must be a simple substance and that there cannot be (the second antinomy), both that there must be at least one first or uncaused cause and that there cannot be (the third antinomy), and that there must be a being whose necessary existence is the ground of all contingent beings and that there can be no necessary being (the fourth antinomy).

The only way of resolving these contradictions, Kant argues, is by accepting that the natural world is a realm of appearance, constituted by the application of the categories to sensible intuitions, and not a realm of things in themselves. Regarding the first two antinomies, which he calls "mathematical" because they have to do with size and duration, Kant argues that there is no fact of the matter about the size of the world as a whole, because the natural world is never present in experience as a whole, but rather is given to us only through the progressive or regressive synthesis of spatiotemporal intuitions. We can always proceed *indefinitely* far in the progressive composition of spaces and times into ever larger or longer realms or in the regressive decomposition of space and time into ever smaller regions, but we can never reach a beginning or an end to such series, as would be possible if they were finite, nor complete any synthesis of them as infinite either. Both sides of the mathematical antinomies, therefore, turn out to be false, because both rest on the false assumption that the world is given independently of our ongoing synthesis in its representation, and therefore has a determinate magnitude, which must be either finite or infinite. For the third and fourth antinomies, which he calls "dynamical" (because they have to do with causation), Kant proposes a different solution. Here he argues that both sides of the apparent contradiction may be true, if the denial (of a free cause or necessary being) is restricted to the natural and sensible world and the affirmation is taken to refer to what might exist in a noumenal or supersensible world of things in themselves. Just as his thinking about the antinomies generally shaped his thinking about the structure and outcome of the entire "Transcendental Dialectic," so Kant's resolution of the third antinomy goes on to play an important role in his moral philosophy, for his practical proof of the reality of our freedom presupposes his theoretical argument for its possibility.

The "Ideal of Pure Reason."   Rational theology, the third and last of the metaphysical pseudosciences, is taken up by Kant in the final chapter of the "Transcendental Dialectic" (A567–642/B595–670). If an "idea" is a pure concept generated by reason, then an "ideal" is the concept of an *individual thing* as exemplifying an idea. It would not be natural to think of the idea of the soul, for example, as giving rise to an ideal, because we naturally think there are many souls; but it is natural (at least in a culture centered on monotheism) to think of the idea of God as the idea of a single being. Kant argues for the inevitability of the idea of God as an *ens realissimum*, or supreme individual thing possessing all realities or perfections and thus also grounding all the possibilities realized by other particular things. Much of Kant's argument here makes use of a line of thought he developed nearly twenty years before the publication of the *Critique*, in *The Only Basis for a Demonstration of the Existence of God* (1763). But now Kant subjects to withering criticism his own earlier attempt to prove the existence of God as well as the other traditional attempts to prove the existence of God, which were already criticized in his earliest philosophical writings.

Kant organizes the traditional proofs of the existence of God into (1) the ontological proof, based solely on the *concept* of God, (2) the *cosmological* proof, based on the mere existence of a world, and (3) the *physicotheological* proof, based on the constitution of the actual world, especially its alleged exhibition of purposive design. The first of these is Kant's representation of the proof offered by Descartes; the second is his name for an argument from contingent existents to their necessary ground found in Wolff and his followers; and the third is what Kant calls the argument from design favored by so many thinkers of the early Enlightenment, especially in Britain. Hume had already both presented it sympathetically and subjected it to searching criticism in his *Dialogues Concerning Natural Religion*; a German translation of Hume's book had not yet been published before Kant finished the *Critique*, but Kant had read a partial translation and précis of it by his friend Johann Georg Hamann.

First Kant attacks the ontological argument, holding that since existence is not a property and therefore not a perfection, it cannot be included among the determinations included in the idea of God, and therefore cannot be inferred from that idea alone. Kant then argues that even if the cosmological and physicotheological proofs could establish the existence of some necessary and purposive being (which he does not concede they can), they still could not establish the existence of a supremely perfect Deity unless the ontological proof also succeeded. Since the ontological proof is unsound, Kant argues, the entire metaphysical enterprise of proving the existence of God as an object of *theoretical cognition* must be abandoned as hopeless.

Regulative use of the ideas.   At this point the outcome of the "Transcendental Dialectic" seems entirely negative. But this is misleading. In an appendix to the "Dialectic," Kant begins a limited rehabilitation of the ideas of traditional metaphysics by arguing that the ideas of reason have an important function in the conduct of natural science if they are understood *regulatively*. That is, they should be taken to represent not metaphysical entities whose reality is demonstrable, but instead goals and directions of inquiry that mark out the ways in which our *empirical* knowledge is to be sought and organized. The idea of a simple soul stimulates us to search for a unified psychology; the idea of a complete world whole leads us constantly to expand the domain of our scientific investigations; and the idea of God guides us in regarding the world as if it were the product of a highest intelligence, which leads us to look for the maximum in order and connectedness in whatever empirical knowledge we do acquire. This argument, which Kant continues in the *Critique of the Power of Judgment*, is the first of Kant's constructive arguments that pure reason, although it can be misleading, is essential to inquiry if wisely used.

"The Doctrine of Method."   The second major division of the *Critique*, the "Doctrine of Method," tends to be neglected by its readers, perhaps because the arguments already surveyed are so exhausting. But in the "Doctrine of Method" Kant reflects upon the potential and the limits of his critical philosophy by comparing it with other methods. He compares the method of philosophy with the method of mathematics, the method of theoretical philosophy with the method of practical philosophy, and the method of critical philosophy with the methods of dogmatic, empirical, and skeptical philosophy. These reflections include some extremely important discussions.

The first chapter, the "Discipline of Pure Reason," provides Kant's most mature treatment of the difference between philosophy and mathematics. It argues that both provide synthetic *a priori* cognition, but that mathematics provides determinate answers to its problems only because its objects can be constructed in pure intuition, whereas philosophy provides only general principles because what it can construct are the conditions of possibility for the experience of objects, not particular objects (A712–38/B740–69). Kant then provides an ardent defense of freedom of public communication as well as of open-mindedness in the discussion of metaphysical issues, arguing that the very existence of reason itself depends on the free give-and-take of controversy between rational beings, which requires the liberty to come to one's own conclusions honestly and to express them openly to others (A738–69/B766–97). The chapter concludes with a discussion of the contrasting roles of hypotheses in science and philosophy (A769–82/B798–810) and then with a reflection upon his own style of philosophical argumentation, what he calls "transcendental proofs" (A782–94/B810–22).

The second chapter of the "Doctrine of Method," the "Canon of Pure Reason," contrasts the epistemological status of theoretical cognition with that of the principles and presuppositions of practical reason, or morality, and in so doing provides Kant's most systematic discussion of moral philosophy prior to the *Groundwork for the Metaphysics of Morals* (1785) and Kant's first systematic statement of his argument for rational faith in God on moral grounds (A795–831/B823–59). This is an argument that Kant was to restate, refine, and develop in the subsequent two critiques and *Religion within the Boundaries of Mere Reason*. The third chapter, the "Architectonic of Pure Reason," continues the discussion of the contrast between philosophy and other forms of cognition, such as historical knowledge, as well as of the contrast within philosophy between theoretical and practical reason (A832–51/B860–79), while the final chapter of the "Doctrine of Method," and of the whole *Critique*, the "History of Pure Reason," orients the critical philosophy clearly in relation to the competing positions of dogmatism, empiricism, skepticism, and indifferentism, the discussion of which had opened the *Critique* (A852–6/B880–4).

2 The Message of the *Critique*

The *Critique of Pure Reason* is complex and many-sided. Both its overall message and its meaning for the subsequent history of philosophy defy easy summary. The *Critique* has perhaps most often been seen as marking out a third way that combines the virtues, while avoiding the pitfalls, of both the "rationalism" of Descartes and Leibniz and the "empiricism" of Locke and Hume. This way of reading the *Critique*, however, even though to some extent suggested by Kant himself, depends on an oversimplified reading of the history of modern philosophy and at the very least on a flawed understanding and an incomplete assessment of the strengths and weaknesses of Kant's modern predecessors. Less controversial is the observation that the *Critique*'s main intention is to find a middle way between traditional metaphysics, especially its attempts to bolster a theistic view of the world with *a priori* rational arguments, and a skepticism that would threaten to undercut the claims of modern natural science along with those of religious metaphysics.

We see this clearly in the way that Kant seeks to carve out for theoretical philosophy a significant but limited domain, distinct from that of empirical knowledge and the opinions of common sense, but excluding the exaggerated claims that have brought metaphysics into disrepute. The *Critique of Pure Reason* belongs to a main tradition in modern philosophy beginning with Descartes that tries to provide an *a priori* philosophical foundation for the methods and broad features of a modern scientific view of nature by an examination of the suitability of human cognitive faculties for the kind of knowledge that modern science aims to achieve. At the same time, Kant tries to save precisely what the dogmatic metaphysicians cannot, by connecting the claims of religious metaphysics to moral practice, and, in the famous words of the second-edition preface, by limiting knowledge in order to make room for faith (Bxxx). But Kant tries to accomplish all these goals, especially the last, in an authentically *Enlightenment* manner, always giving first place to our rational capacity to reflect on our cognitive abilities and achievements, to correct them, and to subject the pretensions of reason to *self*-limitation, so that human reason itself retains ultimate authority over all matters of human knowledge, belief, and action.

In the seventeenth and eighteenth centuries, the principle of causation had been put into ever more successful use by practicing scientists, but at the same time doubt had been cast upon it by philosophers. First the principle had been supported upon theological foundations by Descartes and his follower Nicolas Malebranche, and then reduced to a mere phenomenon, as by Leibniz, or finally exposed by Hume as merely the psychological result of mere custom. Hume seeks to support the idea of necessary connection, while at the same time depriving it of any objective foundation. Kant, however, argues that a genuine necessary connection between events is required for their objective succession in time, and that the concept of causality in which this connection is expressed is imposed on experience by our own thought as an indispensable condition of its possibility. The human understanding, therefore, is the true lawgiver of nature, and the successes of modern science are due to its conduct of its inquiries in accordance with a plan whose ground lies *a priori* in the structure of human thought (Bxii–xviii).

The originality of the *Critique* can be indicated by focusing on the way it attempts simultaneously to resolve two of the most intractable problems of early modern philosophy, the simultaneous vindication of the principle of universal causality and of the freedom of the human will. The great idea of the *Critique of Pure Reason* is that the very thing that explains the possibility of our knowledge of nature is also the key to the possibility of our freedom in both intention and action, the very thing that seems threatened by the rule of causality in that natural world. Kant argues that the principles of the scientific worldview can be known with certainty because they express the structure of our own thought. Thus certitude about the principles of science is possible only because they rest on human autonomy: We are not merely passive perceivers but also cognitive agents who structure what we perceive in accordance with the necessary conditions of our active thought. Thus Kant argues that we can be certain of the fundamental principles of science – above all the universal law of causation – precisely because this law is a condition of the possibility of the thought that we must impose upon our perceptions in order to have any experience at all.

According to Kant, if we understand the principle of causality and the fundamental principles of the scientific worldview as products of our own thought imposed upon experience, this leaves open the possibility of a radical self-determination of human action when the human will is considered not as it appears but as it is in itself. In later works, such as the *Critique of Practical Reason* and the *Religion within the Boundaries of Mere Reason*, Kant completes this theory with the further argument that only the inexorable awareness of our obligation to live up to the moral law, which is given spontaneously by our own reason and which we all acknowledge (even if only in the breach), can prove the reality of our freedom, which is the necessary condition of the possibility of the moral demand we make upon ourselves. Yet this further argument presupposes the first *Critique*'s argument that we cannot ground the principles of natural science themselves without at the same time revealing that their scope is limited to mere appearances.

Kant's bold attempt to resolve with one stroke two of the most pressing problems of modern philosophy has seldom been accepted by his successors, even the most sympathetic among them, without some qualification. Some feel that Kant's identification of the basic principles of science with the fundamental principles of human understanding itself betrays too much confidence in the specifically Newtonian mechanistic physics that prevailed at his time, leaving too little room for subsequent scientific developments, such as the theory of general relativity and quantum mechanics. Others have felt that Kant's reduction of the laws of science to the laws of human thought is not an adequate account of the truly objective validity of science. Few have felt comfortable with the idea that the possibility of freedom can be defended only by rendering the relation between freedom and nature incomprehensible to us. Many have felt that the idea that human freedom is our ultimate value but that it can be realized only through adherence to law is both strange and paradoxical. Yet at the same time, broad elements of Kant's philosophy have become indispensable and therefore often almost invisible assumptions of the modern frame of mind. No modern thinker can believe that the human mind is only a passive recorder of external fact, or a mere "mirror of nature."[4] But although many hold that since we have no way of stepping outside the human point of view, it may not be as easy as Kant thought to separate out our subjective contributions to the constitution of nature. Yet every modern philosophy holds in some form or other the Kantian thesis that human beings make an active contribution to their knowledge. Though few defend human freedom by saying only that it is logically compatible with natural causation, even fewer have thought that the assumption of causal determinism in science precludes conceiving of ourselves as agents who make decisions according to what seem to us to be the most rational

---

4. See Richard Rorty, *Philosophy and the Mirror of Nature* (Princeton, NJ: Princeton University Press, 1979).

principles of value. Thus many have accepted in some form the Kantian idea that there is a difference between the standpoints of actor and spectator.[5] Even those who reject Kant's solutions to the problems of grounding natural science and making sense of moral agency must find a way to avoid what they find objectionable in Kant's solution to them. In this way, all modern thinkers are children of Kant, whether they are happy or bitter about their paternity.

3 Kant's Development toward the *Critique*

The *Critique of Pure Reason* has often been represented as the product of a violent revolution in Kant's thought that took place around 1772 – a midlife crisis in which the forty-eight-year-old thinker rejected his previous adherence to the Leibnizian-Wolffian philosophy, the systematic philosophy that Christian Wolff had created out of the brilliant fragments that were all that was then known of the philosophy of Gottfried Wilhelm Leibniz and that had become the dominant philosophy in enlightened German universities after the 1720s. Kant himself gave rise to this legend with several of his own remarks, above all his comment in the introduction to his *Prolegomena to Any Future Metaphysics* (P) – the short work that he published in 1783 to try to overcome the initially indifferent or hostile reception of the *Critique* – that "it was the recollection of David Hume that many years ago first interrupted my dogmatic slumber and gave an entirely different direction to my investigations in the field of speculative philosophy" (P 4: 260). But this remark may have been less an accurate autobiographical report than it was a way of persuading some of his audience to adopt the standpoint of his critical philosophy, by going through the process that Kant (perhaps only fictionally) represents himself as having followed, for there is no identifiable point in his intellectual history that corresponds to it. There were certainly major changes in Kant's thought both before and after the publication of his inaugural dissertation, *De mundi sensibilis atque intelligibilis forma et principiis* ("On the Form and Principles of the Sensible and Intelligible World"), in 1770, the last publication preceding the years of intense but unpublished work leading up to the publication of the *Critique* in 1781. But Kant has certainly misled those who have supposed that all his work in the years preceding this point was slumbering in Wolffian dogmatism, and that he awoke from this slumber only through some sudden recollection of the skepticism of David Hume.

In fact, Kant had been chipping away at fundamental tenets of the Leibnizian-Wolffian synthesis at least since the publication of his first exclusively philosophical work, his MA thesis *Principiorum primorum cognitionis metaphysicae nova*

5. See Lewis White Beck, *The Actor and the Spectator* (New Haven: Yale University Press, 1975).

dilucidatio ("A New Elucidation of the First Principles of Metaphysical Cognition") in 1755. There were certainly major developments in the content of Kant's philosophical views in the period around 1769–70 leading to the publication of the inaugural dissertation, and then further developments in Kant's doctrines and his conception of philosophical method in the period beginning in 1772 and culminating in the publication of the *Critique*. Many of these were revolutionary developments both in Kant's own thought and in the history of Western philosophy. Even so, the *Critique of Pure Reason*, as well as the further "critical" works that were to follow it, have to be seen as the product of a continuous evolution since at least 1755, a process in which Kant never fully subscribed to the Wolffian orthodoxy and in which he continued revising his position both substantively and methodologically until he arrived at the *Critique*.

Moreover, even after the *Critique* was first published, Kant's thought continued to evolve, and there are major differences between the first and second editions of the work. Indeed, even after the publication of the second edition, Kant continued to revise and refine both his views and his arguments, in published work such as the *Critique of the Power of Judgment* and in the manuscripts on which he was still working at the end of his life (later published as the *Opus postumum*). Further, it should by no means be thought that Kant's mature philosophy, as first expressed in the *Critique of Pure Reason*, represents an outright rejection of the philosophy of his predecessors, above all of the original philosophy of Leibniz. On the contrary, Kant's philosophy can be thought of as an attempt to synthesize Leibniz's vision of the pre-established harmony of the principles of nature and the principles of grace[6] with the substance of Newtonian science and the moral and political insights of Jean-Jacques Rousseau (1712–78). To the extent that Kant was a critic of the Leibnizian-Wolffian philosophy, his criticisms came not only from Hume but even more from Wolff's Pietist critic Christian August Crusius (1715–75). These critical forerunners led Kant to transform Leibniz's vision of a harmonious world of monads under the rule of God and Rousseau's vision of a social contract expressing a general will into ideals of human reason, neither of which can simply be asserted to exist in well-founded cognitive judgments made within the limits of human sensibility and understanding, but both of which can and must represent the ultimate even if never completely attainable goals of human theoretical and practical thought and conduct.

After a survey of some of the steps toward the *Critique* that Kant took in works published before 1770, the rest of this section will focus on the major

---

6. Leibniz's essays on "The Principles of Nature and Grace" and "Monadology" were written in 1714 and published posthumously in 1718 and 1720; both were known to Kant.

steps that Kant took in the inaugural dissertation of that year and then during the "silent decade" from 1770 until the publication of the *Critique* in 1781. This discussion of the genesis of the *Critique* is provided to help interpret the intentions of the work as well as to cast some light on the complexities of its organization and argumentation.

Nova dilucidatio **(1755).**   In his first treatise on metaphysics, Kant already took issue with some of the most fundamental tenets of the Leibnizian-Wolffian philosophy, while expressing his continued allegiance to other aspects of it. Several of the most important criticisms that Kant made in this first philosophical work would reappear in the *Critique*. Kant made four important critical points in the *Nova dilucidatio* (NE). First, he rejected the assumption, to which Wolff may have been more clearly committed than Leibniz, that there is a "unique, absolutely first, universal principle of all truths" (NE 1: 388). Kant argues here a logical point, that affirmative truths rest on the principle "whatever is, is" and that negative truths rest on the principle "whatever is not, is not" (NE 1: 389). That is, he argues that the assumption that the negation of a true proposition is false is itself a substantive presupposition of a logical system and not something provable by any logical system itself. This is not yet the argument that there are some truths that can be demonstrated from adequate definitions by logic alone and others that require going beyond logic, which will become the distinction between analytic and synthetic judgments. But it shows that from the outset of his career Kant rejected the supposition that all philosophical truth could in principle be derived from a single principle that lay beneath Leibniz's theory that all true propositions can be proved by the analysis of concepts.

Second, Kant rejected the proofs of the principle of sufficient reason offered by Wolff and Baumgarten. According to Kant, their proof was that if it were assumed that something did not have a sufficient ground, then its sufficient ground would be nothing, which would then mean that nothing was something (NE 1: 397); this is both circular, assuming precisely what is in question (that everything does have a ground), and also a mere play on words. Kant's alternative argument is that in every true proposition the subject must be determinate with respect to any predicate that might be asserted of an object, so that there must always be something that determines whether a given predicate is true of it (NE 1: 393–4). This is not adequate either, since it fails to see that nothing more than the *properties* of an object are necessary to determine what *predicates* should be asserted of it. But it already reveals Kant's characteristic tendency to convert *ontological* questions into *epistemological* questions – that is, the transformation of questions about what sorts of things there must be into questions about the conditions under which it is possible for us to make claims to knowledge about things. The development of this tendency into a full-blown philosophical method will be the key to the *Critique of Pure Reason*, in which, as Kant is to say, "The proud name of ontology, which presumes to offer synthetic *a priori* cognition of things in general in a systematic doctrine . . . must give way to the modest one of a mere analytic of pure understanding" (A247/B303).

Third, Kant rejected the argument which he was later famously to dub the "ontological" argument for the existence of God. This was the proof of St. Anselm, revived by Descartes and refined by Leibniz, that the existence of God could be inferred from predicates necessarily included in the concept of God. Kant's rejection of it was based on the supposition that its proof is "ideal" rather than "real": that is, that it only unpacks what we may have included in the *concept* of God but cannot establish that there is any *object* answering to that concept (NE 1: 394–5). At this stage, Kant offered an alternative argument that the real existence of God must be accepted as the ground of all *possibility*. He would reject this argument too in the *Critique of Pure Reason*, but his hostility to the ontological argument and his analysis of its defect were to remain essentially unchanged. His criticism of the ontological argument was another precursor of the *Critique of Pure Reason*'s foundational distinction between analytic and synthetic judgments. In the *Critique*, Kant will argue that all substantive truths in mathematics, physical science, and philosophy itself, although necessarily true and knowable independently of appeal to any particular experience (what he will call "*a priori*"), go beyond what can be derived from the mere analysis of concepts, and therefore require the discovery of a whole new method of thought beyond the method of analysis employed by his predecessors Leibniz, Wolff, and Baumgarten.

Finally, in the *Nova dilucidatio* Kant rejects the basic principle of Leibniz's monadology. This is the principle that everything true of a substance is true in virtue of the inherent nature of that substance itself, so that what would appear to be real interactions between substances are only reflections of the harmonious plan God has chosen to follow as the creator of all substances in a world that is the best of all possible ones precisely because it is harmonious. Kant maintains what he calls the "Principle of Succession," that "No change can happen to substances except insofar as they are connected with other substances; their reciprocal dependency on each other determines their reciprocal changes of state" (NE 1: 410). Kant used this principle to argue for the system of "physical influx," which his teacher Martin Knutzen (1713–51) had defended against the monadology. The argument for a system of real interaction among all physical objects in space and time would become a crucial part of the "principles of empirical thought" for which Kant would argue in the *Critique*. Further, Kant also derived from this "principle of succession" a special argument that all changes among *perceptions* would have to be explained as due to changes in *bodies*, and thus a proof of the "real existence of bodies" (NE 1: 411–12). Changed from an ontological to an epistemological key, this argument would become the basis of the "Refutation of Idealism" in the second edition of the *Critique of Pure Reason*.

So Kant's first publication in philosophy already contained some of his most characteristic criticisms of his predecessors as well as some of the substantive conclusions of his mature work. What was still needed was a new philosophical method that could get him beyond his own still shaky arguments for these conclusions to a totally new foundation for them. That would take at least two more decades to discover. Meanwhile, in the *Nova dilucidatio*, Kant still agreed with Leibniz on one point that he would only later reject: Leibniz's position on freedom of the will. At this stage, Kant recognized only the two traditional alternatives of determinism, according to which any event, including a human action, is entirely determined by an antecedent sequence of events, which in the case of a human action may go all the way back to earlier involuntary events in the agent's life or before, and indeterminism, according to which a free human choice is in no way determined by any prior history. The latter position, which Kant called the "indifference of equilibrium," was represented for him by Crusius and firmly rejected on the ground that this position would undermine any reasonable conception of responsibility. Instead, Kant opted for Leibniz's position, a form of determinism now known as "compatibilism": All events, including human actions, admit of causal explanation, but some human actions are due to an inner rather than an outer cause or principle, and among those some are due to the representation of the chosen action as what would be best for the agent to do. Actions caused in this way, even though they might be necessary and predictable, are still entitled to be called spontaneous, voluntary, or free (NE 1: 402). By the time of the *Critique of Practical Reason*, Kant was to reject this Leibnizian conception of freedom as the "freedom of a turnspit" (CPrR 5: 97), and it was to be a fundamental task of the *Critique of Pure Reason*, not yet foreseen in 1755, to make way for a third alternative between traditional determinism and indeterminism. Kant would do this by means of his transcendental idealism, his distinction between the necessary appearance of things to human cognition and how those things, including human agents themselves, might be in themselves: This would allow him to treat as at least logically consistent both Leibnizian and Crusian positions. The Leibnizian position might be the truth about appearances or "phenomena," while the Crusian position might be true about things in themselves, or "noumena."

The philosophical works of 1762–64.   The next period of major philosophical publication for Kant was the years 1762 to 1764, during which time he published four philosophical works all of which are important stepping stones to the *Critique of Pure Reason*. Three of these works appear to have been completed in the fall of 1762, possibly in this order: the *False Subtlety of the Four Syllogistic Figures* (FS), published in 1762; *The Only Possible Basis for a Demonstration of the Existence of God* (OPA), published in 1763; and the *Inquiry Concerning the Distinctness of the Principles of Natural Theology and Morality* (NTM), the second-prize winner in a competition held by the Berlin Academy of Sciences, in which an "Essay on Evidence" by Moses Mendelssohn (1729–85) won first prize. Finally, the *Attempt to Introduce the Concept of Negative Magnitudes into Philosophy* was completed and published by the summer of 1763.

The essay on *False Subtlety*, which was primarily concerned to effect a simplification of the many classes of syllogism recognized in Aristotelian logic, would seem to contribute the least to the emergence of the *Critique of Pure Reason*. But in its "Concluding Reflection" Kant touches on one theme that would become crucial for both the formulation as well as the solution of virtually all the philosophical problems dealt with in the *Critique*. This is the claim that the fundamental notion in formal logic and in the analysis of the powers of the human capacity for cognition is the notion of *judgment*. Concepts, Kant argues, which link predicates to one another can become distinct only by means of judgments; and inferences, which might have been thought to call upon additional powers of mind beyond the power of judgment, are in fact complex or iterated judgments (FS 2: 58–9). Thus Kant concludes that "*understanding* and *reason*, that is to say, the faculty of cognizing distinctly and the faculty of syllogistic reasoning, are not different *fundamental faculties*. Both consist in the capacity to judge" (FS 2: 59). The recognition that judgment is the fundamental form of all cognitive acts will be crucial to the *Critique* in three ways. First, Kant will formulate the problem of the very possibility of philosophy as the problem of the possibility of synthetic *a priori* judgment, or the problem of how judgments can go beyond what can be derived from the mere analysis of concepts yet also claim universal and necessary validity. Second, he will argue that the necessary conditions for the application of categories derived from the logical forms of judgment to the spatiotemporal form of human experience are the source of all those synthetic *a priori* judgments that theoretical (as contrasted to practical or moral) philosophy can actually prove. Finally, he will argue, in the "Transcendental Dialectic" of the first *Critique*, that the fundamental illusion of traditional metaphysics is to think that human reason gives direct theoretical insight into the constitution of things as they are in themselves instead of simply concatenating simpler judgments of the understanding into

the more complex judgments we call syllogisms or inferences and forming
nondemonstrable ideas on the basis of these inferences. Kant's insistence on
the primacy of judgment in human thought is a first step toward all these
critical theses.

In *The Only Possible Basis for a Demonstration of the Existence of God*,
Kant's thought advanced toward the *Critique* from a different direction. The
argument of this book divides into two main parts. In the first section, as the title
suggests, Kant discusses proofs of the existence of God. On the one hand, he
refines his criticism of the ontological argument, and adds to it criticisms of two
other traditional arguments, the argument from the contingency of the world to
the necessity of its cause, which had been popularized by Leibniz and which
Kant named the "cosmological" argument, and the argument from the order of
the world to an intelligent author of it, or the argument from design, which was
widely popular among eighteenth-century thinkers and which Kant called the
"physicotheological" argument. On the other hand, Kant refines his own argument that the existence of God can be demonstrated as an actual and necessary
condition of the existence of any other possibility, an argument that appeals to
the premise that it would be impossible to deny that anything is possible (OPA 2:
79). From the concept of God as the necessary ground of possibility, Kant then
proceeds to derive traditional predicates of God such as uniqueness, simplicity,
immutability, and indeed even the claim that the necessary being is a mind (OPA
2: 83–7). The second main section of the *Only Possible Basis* shows Kant's
early concern to find a proper characterization of scientific laws of nature, and
reveals that Kant's complex view of teleology, or final causes, which seems to
be a late accretion to the *Critique of Pure Reason*, touched on only in the
appendix to the "Transcendental Dialectic" (A642–704/ B670–732) and fully
developed only in the *Critique of the Power of Judgment* (CJ), was actually
a longstanding part of his thought. Thus Kant argues "That in the procedure of
purified philosophy there prevails a rule which, even if it is not formally stated,
is nonetheless always observed in practice . . . that in investigating the causes of
certain effects one must pay careful attention to maintaining the unity of nature
as far as possible" (OPA 2: 113). Here Kant defined an ideal of human knowledge that would become central to the *Critique of Pure Reason* and all of his
subsequent works, even as its theological foundation in a conception of God
became ever more attenuated. To have knowledge of the events of an objective
world beyond one's own consciousness is to subsume those events under causal
laws, and to have knowledge of causal laws is to conceive of those laws as
themselves part of a system of laws that, if not actually created by God, can
nevertheless only be conceived by us as if they had been created by an intelligence like but more powerful than ours (see CJ 5: 180). Although Kant did not

yet see how much effort this would involve, his task in the *Critique of Pure Reason* and subsequent works would be precisely to show that knowledge of the "unity of nature" or of constant laws of nature is the necessary condition of the unity of our own experience, and to explain how knowledge of such laws of nature itself is possible.

Kant wrote the *Inquiry Concerning the Distinctness of the Principles of Natural Theology and Morality* in the late fall of 1762 for the Prussian Academy of Science competition on the question of whether metaphysics, conceived to include natural theology and ethics, had the same prospects for certitude as mathematics and could use the same method. The Academy, dominated by Wolffians, preferred Moses Mendelssohn's elegant restatement of the fundamental tenets of Wolffianism for the first prize, but recognized the merits of Kant's essay with an honorable mention and publication along with Mendelssohn's essay (which took place in 1764).

Kant's most radical departure from prevailing orthodoxy in this work comes in his account of mathematical certainty. Instead of holding that mathematics proceeds by the two-step process of analyzing concepts and then confirming the results of those analyses by comparison with our experience, Kant argues that in mathematics definitions of concepts, no matter how similar they may seem to those current in ordinary use, are artificially constructed by a process which he for the first time calls "synthesis," and that mathematical thinking gives itself objects "*in concreto*" for these definitions, or *constructs* objects for its own concepts from their definitions. Thus, whatever exactly the concept of a cone might signify in ordinary discourse, in mathematics the concept of a cone "is the product of the arbitrary representation of a right-angled triangle which is rotated on one of its sides" (NTM 2: 276). We can have certain knowledge of the definition because we ourselves construct it, and we can have certain knowledge that the definition correctly applies to its objects because the true objects of mathematics are only objects constructed in accordance with the definitions that we ourselves have constructed. However, while "geometers acquire their concepts by means of *synthesis* ... Philosophers can acquire their concepts only by means of *analysis* – and that completely changes the method of thought" (NTM 2: 289). Further, while from the definitions introduced into mathematics determinate objects can be constructed, this is not the case in philosophy, where the objects of knowledge are not our own constructs, and where our concepts give us only abstract and indeterminate knowledge of objects rather than determinate and concrete objects themselves. Mathematical knowledge is certain because it is grounded on definitions of our own construction and fully determinate because concrete objects can be constructed from those

definitions, but philosophical knowledge is less certain because it is dependent on the analysis of given concepts and less determinate because it yields
only general judgments about objects.

Kant is here clearly working his way toward several of the central ideas of the
Critique of Pure Reason. Although he does not yet speak of analytic or synthetic
judgments, his distinction between analytic and synthetic *methods* is leading in
that direction: Whereas traditionally this contrast between methods was merely
a contrast between direction in causal or syllogistic inference, for Kant the
difference has become one between constructing concepts or their definitions
(the synthetic method) and unpacking concepts to get to definitions (the analytical method). This will lead to the distinction between judgments that construct
fuller concepts by amplifying what is given (synthetic judgments) and those that
merely explicate given concepts by showing what predicates they already
contain (analytic judgments) (see A6–7). Kant further argues in this essay that
both metaphysics and morality depend upon indemonstrable material principles, and not just formal or logical principles, thereby preparing the way for
the fundamental tenet of his mature theoretical and practical philosophy that the
basic propositions of both are synthetic yet *a priori* judgments. But Kant's
conception of philosophical method in the *Inquiry* has not yet caught up to this
recognition: He is at a loss to explain how we know these "indemonstrable"
principles when the method of philosophy is still considered to be analytic,
rather than synthetic like the method of mathematics. Before Kant's mature
work could be written, he would have to discover a philosophical method that
could yield "material" or synthetic judgments. This would be the philosophical
work of the 1770s that would finally pave the way for the *Critique of Pure
Reason*.

The last of the essays of 1762–64, the *Attempt to Introduce the Concept of
Negative Magnitudes into Philosophy* (NM), focuses on a substantive rather
than a methodological issue. Kant considers a variety of relationships that
must be construed as real opposition rather than logical contradiction: positive and negative numbers, motion in opposite directions, pleasure and pain.
Asserting a proposition and its contradictory results in a contradiction, which
asserts nothing at all. Combining equal motions in opposite directions does
not result in a logical nonentity, but in a state of rest that is a real state of
affairs. So all sorts of sciences need room for the concept of positive and
negative magnitudes, not just the logical notion of contradiction. Kant's
thought here is again that the formal, logical laws of identity and contradiction are not sufficient principles for knowledge of the objective world, and
that philosophy must find room for material principles. He concludes by
noting that the relation between cause and effect, although it is not

a relation of opposition, is also a real rather than a logical relation, and cannot be justified by any mere analysis of concepts showing that the consequence is contained in the ground. This raises the fundamental question, "How am I to understand **the fact that, because something is, something else** is?" (NM 2: 202). The problem of understanding real opposition, real causation, and more generally real relations becomes the fundamental substantive problem of theoretical philosophy. Kant rejects Crusius's attempt to solve this problem (NM 2: 203), and makes no mention of Hume's formulation of an empirical solution to this problem, which was already available to him in the German translation of the first *Enquiry* (1755). But he concludes with these prophetic words:

> Let us see whether we can offer a distinct explanation of how it is that, **because something is, something else is canceled,** and whether we can say anything more than I have already said on the matter, namely that it simply does not take place in virtue of the law of contradiction. I have reflected upon the nature of our cognition with respect to our judgment concerning grounds and consequences, and one day I shall present a detailed account of the fruits of my reflections. (NM 2: 203–4)

This day was not to come until the publication of the *Critique of Pure Reason* in May 1781; Kant had identified a problem to which he did not yet possess a solution. But he clearly was not waiting for a recollection of Hume to awake him from dogmatic slumbers.

The inaugural dissertation (1770).   Kant's last work on the way to the *Critique* before the "silent decade" of the 1770s was his inaugural dissertation (ID), *De Mundi Sensibilis atque Intelligibilis Forma et Principiis* ("On the Form and Principles of the Sensible and Intelligible World"), defended and published in August 1770, after Kant's long-awaited ascension to the chair of logic and metaphysics in Königsberg. This work is a milestone in Kant's progress toward the *Critique of Pure Reason* because it introduces the fundamental distinction between the sensible and the intellectual capacities of the mind: the capacity, on the one hand, to have singular and immediate representations of particular objects by means of the senses, which Kant henceforth calls "intuition" (*intuitus, Anschauung*), and, on the other hand, the capacity to form abstract and general representations, or concepts, by means of the intellect. Further, as his title suggests, Kant argues that our capacities for intuition and conceptualization each have their own characteristic forms, principles, or laws, which can be known by us and which constitute the basis of metaphysical cognition. Moreover, Kant argues, introducing the doctrine that he will later name "transcendental idealism," the *"laws of intuitive cognition"* (ID 2: 388), or the laws of the representation of things by means of the senses, characterize how things necessarily *appear* to us, but not how they actually are in themselves (ID 2: 392). By contrast, at this stage, although not later, Kant holds that intellectual representations of things, or concepts, present things "*as they are.*" Thus, sensibility and intellect present us with two different accounts of objects: "phenomena," things as they appear to the senses, and "noumena," things as they really are and are known to be by the intellect (*nous*). Here Kant uses the term in what he will later call a "positive" rather than permissible "negative" sense (B307).

On this account, sensibility and the intellect operate essentially independently of one another. The fundamental stimulus to this radical distinction seems to have been Kant's discovery, perhaps made in 1769, that several paradoxes about the infinite, such as the conflict between the supposition that time appears to have no beginning yet any object and thus any universe of objects must have had a beginning, could be resolved by distinguishing between the forms of intuition as forms of appearance, on the one hand, and the forms of thought as the forms of reality, on the other: Thus it could be argued, for example, that there is no contradiction between the sensible appearance that time has no beginning and the reality, known by the intellect, that all existence must have some beginning, for sensibility and intellect do not present the same things. In the *Critique of Pure Reason*, Kant was to call the set of such paradoxes, to be resolved by the distinction between phenomena and noumena, the antinomies of pure reason.

However, there is also a crucial difference between Kant's treatment of the antinomies in 1770 and his eventual treatment of them in 1781. This is connected with an equally fundamental difference in Kant's conception of the relation between the two basic mental capacities of intuition and conceptualization in the inaugural dissertation and the *Critique*. In the dissertation, Kant supposes that the intellect alone reveals the true nature of reality, and that the antinomies are to be resolved by preventing any limits inherent in the laws of sensibility from being misconstrued as limits on purely intellectual knowledge of reality. But he has in fact no adequate account of the role of concepts in knowledge of ordinary objects in space and time, and once he realizes – as he will after 1772 – that concepts of the understanding must be used in conjunction with the intuitions or data supplied by sensibility to account for the possibility of such knowledge, not independently, then he will also have to revise his account of the antinomies. In the *Critique* he will have to revise his resolution of them by arguing that there can be no knowledge of any spatiotemporal reality at all beyond the limits of sensibility, although in cases where concepts of the understanding can be used to formulate coherent conceptions of nonspatiotemporal entities, above all God but also our own freedom, there may be coherent *belief* (rational assent on practical grounds) even if never *knowledge*.

In sum, in the inaugural dissertation Kant introduces his fundamental distinction between intuitions and concepts, and uses that distinction for a resolution of the antinomies, but does not yet realize that knowledge can arise only from the conjoint use of intuitions and concepts to yield a unified experience. Once he comes to that realization, he will have to transform his resolution of the antinomies, surrendering the view that sensibility gives us knowledge of appearances and the intellect metaphysical knowledge of things as they are in themselves. Only then will the way be open for Kant's fully mature position that the limits of knowledge leave room for certain beliefs that cannot become knowledge but that can be justified on practical grounds (see Bxxiv–xxx).

In particular, section 3 of the dissertation presents a treatment of the forms of intuition, space and time, that will be carried over into the *Critique* largely unaltered, although (especially in the second edition of the *Critique)* somewhat amplified. Here Kant claims that the principle of form of the world as appearance or phenomenon is "a fixed law of the mind, in virtue of which it is necessary that all the things that can be objects of the senses ... are seen as *necessarily* belonging to the same whole" (ID 2: 398). He then argues that there are in fact two such laws or principles: time, the form of all that we sense, whether inner or outer, and space, the form of our outer sense, or our sensory perception of objects we take to be distinct from ourselves. Kant argues that space and time are both the *pure forms* of all intuitions, or "*formal principle*[*s*] *of the sensible world*" (ID 2: 402), and themselves *pure intuitions* (ID 2: 399): They are the forms in which particular objects are presented to us by the senses, but also themselves unique particulars of which we can have *a priori* knowledge, the basis of our *a priori* knowledge of both mathematics and physics (ID 2: 397–8). But the embrace of space and time "is limited to *actual things,* insofar as they are thought capable of *falling under the senses*" – we have no ground for asserting that space and time characterize things that we are incapable of sensing; indeed, we must deny it (ID 2: 398).

Kant makes the following claims about time (ID 2: 398–402): (1) "*The idea of time does not arise from but is presupposed by the senses*"; this is because any concepts we can form from our experience of things already presupposes that we can represent them as either simultaneous or successive. (2) "*The idea of time is singular* and not general"; this is because all particular times, say two particular years, are thought of as part of a single larger time, in which they each occupy a determinate position, and are not just unrelated tokens of a similar type. (3) "*The idea of time is an intuition*," and indeed a "*pure intuition*," precisely because it is both singular and immediately given to us in all our experience, which makes it an intuition, but also given to us as presupposed by rather than abstracted from all our experience, which makes it pure. All of these claims will be reiterated in the *Critique of Pure Reason* (A30–2/B46–8).

Next, Kant asserts a claim that is not explicitly made in the initial discussion of time in the *Critique* but is presupposed in a number of later important parts of the work: (4) *"Time is a continuous magnitude,"* or consists of no simple parts but instead between any two times, no matter how small, there is always another, smaller interval of time. Then Kant argues that (5) *"Time is not something objective and real,* nor is it a substance, nor an accident, nor a relation." There is both a positive and a negative aspect to this claim. The positive side is the argument that we must have a pure intuition of time because it is presupposed by our perception of any particular objects or states as simultaneous or successive, the argument (1) which Kant now reiterates. This implies that we must have a pure representation of time independent of any particular empirical perception, but it does not imply that time is not also "objective and real," that is, *nothing but a form of representation.* For that further, negative claim Kant suggests two sorts of reasons. First he aims a metaphysical objection against Newton and "the English philosophers," namely that the idea of absolute time as a substance or a property of any substance (such as the *sensorium dei*) is absurd. Then he aims an epistemological argument against Leibniz, namely that conceiving of time as something we abstract from perceived relations of objects would render our knowledge of it merely empirical and therefore "completely destroy" all the certitude of the fundamental rules of mathematics and physics. The full premises of this epistemological argument, however, are not spelled out before the *Critique,* and even there are only hinted at (A46–9/B64–7). Finally, Kant adds that although (6) *"time,* posited in itself and absolutely, would be an imaginary being," nevertheless, as "the universal form of phenomena," whether inner or outer, it is "to the highest degree true" and (7) "an absolutely first *formal principle of the sensible world."*

Kant makes a series of parallel claims about space (ID 2: 402–5). He claims (1) *"The concept of space is not abstracted from outer sensations,"* because I can "only conceive of something as placed outside me [*extra me*] by representing it as in a place which is different from the place in which I am myself." In other words, I cannot abstract the concept of space from my experience of objects distinct from myself because I cannot experience them as distinct without already representing them as in space. (2) Like that of time, *"the concept of space is a singular representation,"* because all regions of space are represented as parts of a single, boundless space rather than as instances of some general sort. As before, Kant infers from these two arguments that (3) *"The concept of space is thus a pure intuition."* It is an intuition because it is singular, and it is pure because it is not "compounded from sensations" but is presupposed by all "outer sensation" or experience of objects as distinct from ourselves. Here Kant skips an argument that space is a continuous quantity, although he will also assume that in the *Critique*, and instead inserts an argument about incongruent counterparts that he had made in 1768, using it now to show that since features of directionality such as a right- and left-handedness are not inferable from the concepts of objects, they must be "apprehended by a certain pure intuition." (This argument will be omitted from the *Critique*.) Now, as in the case of time, Kant infers from these results that "*Space is not something objective and real*, nor is it a substance, nor an accident, nor a relation; it is rather, subjective and ideal; it issues from the nature of the mind." Again, he infers this from the prior arguments that it is "the scheme ... for coordinating everything that it senses externally" and also from the two additional claims, the metaphysical claim made against "the English" that the idea of "an *absolute* and boundless *receptacle* of possible things is absurd" and the epistemological argument made against Leibniz that conceiving of the propositions of geometry, which are taken to describe space, as merely abstracted from an experience of relations among objects would "cast geometry down from the summit of certainty, and thrust it back into the rank of those sciences of which the principles are empirical." Finally, Kant again concludes that, even though (5) "the *concept of space* as some objective and real being or property be imaginary, nonetheless, *relatively to all sensible things whatever*, it is not only a concept that is in the highest degree true, it is also the foundation of all truth in outer sensibility." This is as good a statement of the doctrine of transcendental idealism as we will find in the *Critique* itself, insisting on both the subjectivity yet also universality and necessity of space as a form of representation (see A28/B44).

Unlike this presentation of transcendental idealism, the final sections of the dissertation present a view of metaphysical knowledge that must still undergo considerable revision. In section 4 of the dissertation Kant gives an account of the "principle of the form of the intelligible world" that is still largely unchanged from his earliest work but will disappear from the *Critique*, namely the Leibnizian argument that a multitude of substances can constitute a single world only in virtue of their common dependence on a single cause. Not only this argument but also the underlying assumption that pure concepts of the intellect, such as the concept of substance, can be used on their own to provide knowledge of things as they are in themselves will disappear from the *Critique*. It will be replaced by Kant's critical position that pure categories of the understanding lead to ideas of reason that are illusory if used for theoretical knowledge on their own, although they can serve as postulates of practical reason. This change will also require a transformation of Kant's treatment of "method in metaphysics" in the concluding section 5 of the inaugural dissertation. Kant begins by arguing that philosophy has no special method to prescribe to ordinary science, because here the use of the intellect is only logical, organizing concepts that are not themselves provided by the intellect but are instead abstracted from experience. In the case of metaphysics, however, where the intellect does have a real use, supplying original concepts, "*method precedes all science*" (ID 2: 410–11). The method of metaphysics, Kant then maintains, "amounts to this prescription: great care must be taken *lest the principles that are native to sensitive cognition transgress their limits, and affect what belongs to the understanding*" (ID 2: 412). The fundamental obstacle to progress in metaphysics, that is, comes from assuming that the necessary conditions and inherent limits of sensibility are limits on the possibility of intellectual knowledge as well. Kant lists three "subreptic axioms" that arise from this confusion. These unwarranted assumptions are:

1. The same sensitive condition, under which alone the *intuition* of an object is possible, is a condition of the *possibility of the object* itself.
2. The same sensitive condition, under which alone *it is possible to compare what is given so as to form a concept of the understanding of the object*, is also a condition of the possibility itself of the object.
3. The same sensitive condition under which alone *the subsumption of* some *object under a given concept of the understanding* is possible is also the condition of the possibility itself of the object. (ID 2: 413)

In other words, at this stage Kant holds that it is a mistake to assume that the characteristic forms and limits of sensible representations and the conditions for the application of concepts to sensible representations limit our metaphysical cognition of objects as they really are. For example, it is an error to assume that whatever exists is located in space and time (ID 2: 213–14), and it is an error to assume that "*every actual multiplicity can be given numerically*" (ID 2: 415). The implication of Kant's argument is that paradoxes may arise in the attempt to derive metaphysical knowledge from the conditions of sensibility.

Finally, Kant concludes the section by mentioning, almost as an afterthought, that there are certain "principles of convenience" (*principia convenientiae*) that are not principles of sensitive cognition but rather rules by means of which "it seems to the intellect itself easy and practical to deploy its own perspicacity." These are the principles that "*all things in the universe take place in accordance with the order of nature*," that "*principles are not to be multiplied beyond what is absolutely necessary*," and that "*nothing material at all comes into being or passes away*" (ID 2: 418). This is a striking list, because it includes two principles – the principle of universal causation and the principle of the conservation of (material) substance – that Kant will later identify as "constitutive" or necessary conditions of the possibility of the experience of objects at all, but another one – the principle of parsimony traditionally called "Ockham's razor" – that is more like what he will later identify as a "regulative" principle, which is not a necessary condition of the possibility of any experience at all but an assumption that we make for various subjective reasons. The fact that Kant could indiscriminately mix what he would later distinguish as constitutive and regulative principles shows that he did not yet have a clear conception of the function of the former as necessary conditions of the possibility of experience, a consequence of the fact that he did not yet have a clear understanding that the pure concepts of the understanding, such as the concepts of causation and substance, can yield knowledge only when applied to data furnished by the faculty of sensibility. Likewise, that he could argue at this stage that metaphysical illusion can be avoided by not letting the conditions of sensibility limit the use of concepts of the intellect shows that he did not yet see that the concepts of the understanding have a cognitive use only in application to sensibility and therefore within its limits, and beyond that can have only a practical use. Before he could progress from the inaugural dissertation to the *Critique of Pure Reason*, Kant would have to develop a new conception of the use of the intellect with distinctions among the sensible use of the understanding, the illusory use of pure theoretical reason, and the reliable use of pure practical reason.

4 The Genesis of the *Critique* Itself

1770–4. After the publication of the dissertation, Kant fell into a prolonged silence broken only by a few minor essays and a series of letters to his student Marcus Herz. Herz had participated in the public defense of Kant's dissertation and was now in Berlin, studying medicine but also in contact with the prominent philosophers of the capital. Aside from these letters, our primary source of information about Kant's thought in these years comes from surviving notes, though presumably these are only a fragment of what Kant actually wrote during this period and have to be used with caution.[7] Fragmentary as they are, these materials cast light on the emergence of some of the most important new arguments of the *Critique*.

---

7. These consist in notes written in Kant's copy of Baumgarten's *Metaphysica* as well as various loose sheets (*lose Blätter*). They are all referred to as "Reflections." They were edited in volumes 17 and 18 of the *Akademie* edition by Erich Adickes, who assigned them a chronological order based on some dated *lose Blätter* and other indicia such as ink, handwriting, etc. Adickes's dating is conjectural, but since much of the original material went missing in the final days of World War II, it cannot be redone.

In the fall of 1770, Herz went off to Berlin with copies of the dissertation for leading intellectuals such as Mendelssohn, Johann Heinrich Lambert (1728–77), and Johann Georg Sulzer (1720–79). By Christmas, all three Berlin philosophers had replied with letters containing essentially the same objection: How could Kant hold time to be a mere appearance with no objective reality when time is the form of inner sense and we all have immediate experience of changes in inner sense regardless of whatever external significance we might impute to those changing internal senses? (*Correspondence* [Corr] 10: 103–11, 111–13, and 113–16).

Lambert initially raises a question about whether Kant's "two ways of knowing," from the senses and the intellect, "are so completely *separated* that they *never* come together," but then discusses in detail only Kant's treatment of time, accepting Kant's arguments that time is singular, continuous, and the object of a pure intuition but objecting to Kant's idealism about time:

> All changes are bound to time and are inconceivable without time. *If changes are real, then time is real*, whatever it may be. *If time is unreal, then no change can be real.* I think, though, that even an idealist must grant at least that changes really exist and occur in his representations, for example, their beginning and ending. Thus time cannot be regarded as something *unreal*. (Corr 10: 107)

Sulzer's briefer letter also raises a problem about time, asserting the position that *duration* must have "a true reality" even if the formal *concept* of time is some sort of abstraction from our experience of real duration (Corr 10: 107); and Mendelssohn too objects that

> For several reasons I cannot convince myself that time is something merely subjective. Succession is after all at least a necessary condition of the representations that finite minds have. . . . Since we have to grant the reality of succession in a representing creature and in its alternations, why not also in the sensible objects, which are the models and prototypes of representations in the world? (Corr 10: 115)

Kant made no immediate reply to this objection, as we know from his letter to Herz of June 7, 1771 (Corr 10: 121–4). He merely asked Herz to apologize to his correspondents by saying that their letters had set him off on a long series of investigations, and then told Herz that he was now occupied with a work that "under the title *The Bounds of Sensibility and Reason* would work out in some detail the relationship of the concepts and laws determined for the sensible world together with the outline of what the nature of the theory of taste, metaphysics, and morality should contain" (Corr 10: 123). In his next pledge, Kant said that he expected to complete the plan of the work shortly.

Kant's next and most famous letter to Herz is dated February 21, 1772. Here Kant reviewed his plan for the work mentioned the previous June, stating that it was to consist of "two parts, a theoretical and a practical," the first of which in turn would consist of "(1) a general phenomenology and (2) metaphysics, but this only with regard to its nature and method," while the second part was to deal with "(1) the universal principles of feeling, taste, and sensuous desire and (2) the basic principles of morality"(Corr 10: 129). However, Kant says, as he thought about the theoretical part – where the "phenomenology" was to have dealt with the limits of sensitive cognition before the purely intellectual foundations of metaphysics were expounded – "I noticed that I still lacked something essential, something that in my long metaphysical studies I, as well as others, had failed to pay attention to and that, in fact, constitutes the key to the whole secret of hitherto still obscure metaphysics." But the fundamental problem that Kant now announced had nothing to do with the objection to his idealism regarding time that the Berlin savants had raised; indeed, although Kant would eventually acknowledge that objection, he would in no way rethink his position about the ideality of time.

Instead, Kant raises a completely different question: "What is the ground of the relation of that in us which we call representation to the object?" This is a puzzle precisely in the case of the relationship of pure concepts of the understanding to objects presented by sensible experience. It is not a puzzle in the case of entirely empirical representations, which are merely caused by their external objects, nor in the case of divine archetypes (or, we may add, human intentions), where the object is merely caused by the antecedent representation. But, Kant now holds, "the pure concepts of the understanding . . . though they must have their origin in the nature of the soul" because they are formulated by us and known "completely *a priori*," must yet apply to objects of sensible experience even though they are neither caused by nor cause the latter (Corr 10: 130–1). Kant now admits that he had completely passed over this question in the inaugural dissertation because he there failed to realize that our pure concepts as well as forms of intuition must be applied to the same objects, the objects of our experience. Thus what must now be explained is "the possibility of such concepts, with which . . . experience must be in exact agreement and which nevertheless are independent of experience." The idea that the pure concepts of the understanding provide knowledge of entities *other than* the spatiotemporal objects of sensibility is now abandoned. Kant does not describe how the possibility and necessity of the agreement of experience with pure concepts of the understanding is to be explained, beyond suggesting that a systematic classification of these "concepts belonging to complete pure reason" or "categories" can be reached by "following a few fundamental laws of the understanding." Nevertheless, Kant was confident that he would be ready to publish the work, which he now for the first time entitled a *Critique of Pure Reason*, in only three months (Corr 10: 132), although Kant had been using the phrase since 1769 (R 3964, 17: 368, and R 4146, 17: 433).[8] In fact, it would be almost nine years before the work with that title appeared. Much of this delay was due to the fact that Kant did not yet have a clear idea of why the categories necessarily apply to objects of experience.

As Kant thought further about this problem, a problem about time would play a key role, although not the problem about the reality of time but rather a problem about how we can make determinate judgments about the order of objective states of affairs or even our own experiences in time. This problem would become the focus of Kant's attention in the several years following the letter to Herz, especially in 1774–75, and would remain central in the *Critique*.

Kant's next report on his progress is in another letter to Herz, written toward the end of 1773 (Corr 10: 143–6). Kant suggests that he is still working on "a principle that will completely solve what has hitherto been a riddle and that will bring the procedure of the understanding that isolates itself under secure and easily applied rules," but nevertheless promises that he will have his book, which he continues to call "a critique of pure reason," ready by the following Easter or shortly after, that is, in the spring of 1774 (Corr 10: 144–5). In Kant's next surviving letter to Herz, however, written three years later in November 1776 (Corr 10: 198–200), we again find him suggesting that he has been held up by difficulties surrounding the fundamental principle of his new position, although he says that he made progress with it the previous September and once again promises the completed book by the following Easter. Yet the following August still finds Kant reporting "a stone in the way of the *Critique of Pure Reason*," although once again he is optimistic that he can get by this obstacle during the following winter (1778). But in April 1778 Kant writes that the rumor that some pages of his book are already at the press is premature, and in August of that year Kant will only say he is "still working indefatigably" on his "handbook."

So for at least five years the completion of the promised book continued to be put off, and there are repeated hints that Kant has still not found the fundamental principle he needed, presumably the one that would answer the fundamental question of 1772. From the letters to Herz, the only one of his known correspondents in this period to whom Kant said anything about his planned book, it might seem as if Kant was making no progress at all. But our other sources reveal that he was indeed working "indefatigably" on the *Critique* throughout this period, and that beginning by April 1774 – in other words, in the vicinity of his first promised Easter completion date – Kant did begin to explore a solution

---

8. "R" introduces the number assigned to each Reflection by Adickes in the *Akademie* edition. These numbers are reproduced in *Notes and Fragments*, where many of these texts are translated.

to his puzzle about why *a priori* concepts of the understanding should necessarily apply to the data presented to us by sensibility and not have any constitutive cognitive use outside of that application.

1774–75. In this period Kant wrote a series of notes that were clearly part of his work on the *Critique*, one of them on the reverse of a letter sent to him on April 28, 1774. Much of this material goes over claims about space and time already established in the inaugural dissertation, but Kant now adds a line of thought that had not previously appeared. He says that the unity of time implies the unity of the self and the determinate position of all objects in time; even more explicitly that the unity of space depends on the unity of the subject and on the ability of the subject to assign representations of objects determinate positions in space; and then suggests that the concepts of the understanding are necessary precisely to achieve such unification of and order among the intuitions of objects presented in the form of time and space. In his words, he asserts:

1. Time is unique [*einig*]. Which means this: I can intuit all objects only in my self and in representations found in my own subject, and all possible objects of my intuition stand in relation to each other in accordance with the special form of this intuition ...
4. All things and all states of things have their determinate position in time. For through the unity of inner sense they must have their determinate relation to all other putative objects of intuition. (R 4673, 17: 636–7)

He then makes parallel claims about space: Space is not only our unique form for representing objects external to ourselves, but is also unified in the sense that every object must be assigned a determinate position in relation to all others in it:

> Space is nothing but the intuition of mere form even without given matter, thus pure intuition. It is a single [*einzelne*] representation on account of the unity of the subject (and the capability), in which all representations of outer objects can be placed next to one another. (R 4673, 17: 638)

Finally, Kant suggests that the use of concepts of the understanding or rules associated with them is the necessary condition of assigning their determinate positions in a unified space and/or time to objects of representations:

> We have no intuitions except through the senses; thus no other concepts can inhabit the understanding except those which pertain to the disposition and order among these intuitions. These concepts must contain what is universal,

> and rules. The faculty of rules *in abstracto:* the learned understanding; *in concreto:* the common understanding. The common understanding has preference in all cases, where the rules must be abstracted *a posteriori* from the cases; but where they have their origin *a priori*, there it does not obtain at all. (R 4673, 17: 640)

This remark presupposes that concepts are used only in application to intuitions, the thesis that Kant had not yet formulated in 1770 but that was to become the hallmark of the *Critique of Pure Reason*, with its famous statement that "Thoughts without content are empty, intuitions without concepts are blind" (A51/B75). It further suggests that the particular function that the *a priori* concepts of the understanding play is to serve as rules for establishing "disposition and order" among intuitions of objects, although Kant does not yet explain why concepts should be necessary for this purpose or how concepts function as rules for this purpose. Finally, Kant suggests that even the ordinary use of abstraction for the production of empirical concepts depends upon the use of the *a priori* concepts of the understanding for the establishment of this "disposition and order," even though these *a priori* concepts may seem "learned" rather than "common." This is an important point, because it implies that the theory of *a priori* concepts to be worked out in the *Critique of Pure Reason* is not, as is sometimes thought, a theory of the foundations of natural science considered as separate from everyday life, but rather a theory of the foundations of science as continuous with all of our knowledge.

Kant spent much effort in the next several years trying to work out his hunch that the categories can be shown to be *a priori* yet necessary conditions of all of our knowledge of objects by showing that their use is the necessary condition of all determinate "disposition and order" of intuitions. Several notes are assigned to the year 1775 because one of them is written on another letter to Kant dated May 20, 1775. Although, as we saw, Kant had been moving toward the idea of a fundamental contrast between logical and real relations throughout the 1760s, it is only in these notes that he first clearly links his philosophical problem about the application of the categories to sensible intuitions with the distinction between judgments that are analytic and those that are synthetic yet *a priori*. Kant asks under what conditions a predicate b can be predicated of an object x that is also subsumed under another predicate a. In some cases, b can be predicated of any x of which a is predicated because the predicate b is already identical to or contained in a, and we have no need to experience or represent any particular x in order to see that. In such cases, a proposition of the form "All x's that are a are also b" would be true in virtue of "the principle of identity and contradiction," or a "merely logical" "principle of form rather than content," that is, it would be analytic (R 4676, 17: 653–4). If, however, the predicates *a* and *b* can be related to each other only through *x*, then the judgment is synthetic: "If I refer both predicates to *x* and only thereby to each other, then it is synthetic," and the predicates are in that case "not in a logical but in a real relation" (R 4676, 17: 654). Kant also says that "In synthetic propositions the relation between the concepts is not really immediate (for this happens only in the case of analytic propositions), rather it is represented in the conditions of their concrete representation in the subject" (R 4674, 17: 644). Kant does not say so explicitly, but he is clearly already assuming that propositions asserting that *a priori* concepts apply to the objects of sensibility will fall into this class of synthetic judgments expressing real relations.

Kant's next step is to argue that there are three different ways in which synthetic judgments may be made. The object *x* by means of which we link predicates *a* and *b* may be constructed in pure intuition, it may simply be given in empirical intuition or appearance, or it may be "the sensible condition of the subject within which a perception is to be assigned its position" (R 4676, 17: 655). Thus "In mathematics, *x* is the construction of *a*, in experience it is the *concretum*, and with regard to an inherent representation or thought in general *x* is the function of thinking in general in the subject" (R 4674, 17: 655). It is clear enough what Kant means by the first two options. In mathematics, synthetic judgments – such as "The sum of the interior angles of a plane triangle equals two right angles" – are made or confirmed by constructing an object satisfying the first predicate ("plane triangle") in pure intuition, and then seeing that the construction satisfies the second predicate as well ("equals two right angles"); such a construction yields a determinate answer (two right angles contain 180 degrees, not 179 or 181) because it is the construction of a particular object, but it yields a result that is *a priori*, because it takes place in pure intuition, the form that determines the structure of all possible triangles or other spatial figures or objects. In ordinary experience, observation establishes synthetic and determinate but only contingent or *a posteriori* propositions because of the appeal to particular experience: A proposition like "My copy of the *Critique* is worn and dog-eared" adds information ("worn and dog-eared") that goes beyond the initial description of the object ("my copy of the *Critique*"), but that additional information can only be asserted of the particular object that is observed, because it has nothing to do with any essential form of appearance. But what does Kant mean by his third case, referred to only by such obscure phrases as "the sensible condition of a subject" or "the function of thinking in general"?

What Kant has in mind is what he hinted at in 1774, namely that there are certain rules necessary for the "disposition and order" of representations conceived of as belonging to a unified self and occupying determinate positions in the space and time in which that self places its representations, and that these rules add general conditions to the concept of any possible object of experience that go beyond the particular features of such objects we may happen to observe and by means of which we may happen to refer to them. He brings together the steps of this argument thus far in this passage:

> In analytic judgments the predicate *b* pertains properly to the concept *a*, in synthetic judgments to the object of the concept, since the predicate *b* is not contained in the concept. However, the object that corresponds to a concept has certain conditions for the application of this concept, i.e., its position *in concreto* ... Now the condition of all concepts is sensible; thus, if the concept is also sensible, but universal, it must be considered *in concreto*, e.g., a triangle in its construction. If the concept does not signify pure intuition, but empirical, then *x* contains the condition of the relative position ... in space and time, i.e., the condition for universally determining something in them. (R 4684, 17: 671)

This is still somewhat obscure, but what Kant is saying is that judgments that are synthetic but also genuinely universal, that is, *a priori*, can be grounded in one of two ways: In the case of mathematics, such judgments are grounded in the construction of a mathematical object; in the other case, such judgments are grounded in the condition of determining the relative position of one object in space and time to others.

Kant also puts this point by saying that what he is looking for are the principles of the *disposition* or *exposition* of appearances, where that means precisely the assignment of each representation to a determinate position in the unified space and time that is the framework for all the representations belonging to a unified self.

> There is in the soul a *principium* of disposition as well as of affection. The appearances can have no other order and do not otherwise belong to the unity of the power of representation except insofar as they are amenable to the common *principio* of disposition. For all appearance with its thoroughgoing determination must still have unity in the mind, consequently be subjected to those conditions through which the unity of representations is possible. Only that which is requisite for the unity of representations belongs to the objective conditions. The unity of apprehension is necessarily connected with the unity of the intuition of space and time, for without this the latter would give no real representation.
>
> The principles of exposition must be determined on the one side through the laws of apprehension, on the other side through the unity of the power of understanding. They are the standard for observation and are not derived from perceptions, but are the ground of those in their entirety. (R 4678, 17: 660)

Kant's argument is that although all particular representations are given to the mind in temporal form, and all representations of outer objects are given to the mind as spatial representations, these representations cannot be linked to each other in the kind of unified order the mind demands, in which each object in space and time has a determinate relation to any other, except by means of certain principles that are inherent in the mind and that the mind brings to bear on the appearances it experiences. These principles will be, or be derived from, the pure concepts of the understanding that have a subjective origin yet necessarily apply to all the objects of our experience, and those concepts will not have any determinate use except in the exposition of appearances. This is the theory that will answer the puzzle Kant raised in his letter to Herz of February 1772, and that will eventually allow him to write the *Critique.*

In particular, Kant suggests that assigning determinate positions to events in time presupposes a framework of principles employing the same categories that in the other passages he has associated with the concept of a subject or of an object:

> Something must always precede an occurrence (condition of perception).
>   All sorts of things can precede an occurrence, but among these there is one from which it always follows.
>   A reality is always attached (to a point in time and that which determines it) to something accompanying it, through which the point in time is determined (condition of perception).
>   All sorts of things can accompany, but among them there is something that is always there.
>   With regard to that which is simultaneous there is always a connection (condition of perception).
>   But it can be accompanied with all sorts of things; however, what is to be considered as objectively connected is a mutual determination of the manifold by one another.
>   If there were not something that always was, thus something permanent, *stabile*, there would be no firm point or determination of the point in time, thus no perception, i.e., determination of something in time.
>   If there were not something that always preceded an occurrence, then among the many things that precede there would be nothing with which that which occurs belongs in a series, it would have no determinate place in the series.
>   Through the rules of perception the objects of the senses are determinable in time; in intuition they are merely given as appearances. In accordance with those rules there is found an entirely different series than that in which the object was given. (R 4681, 17: 665–6)

Here Kant suggests that what he has previously called the "exposition of appearances" is the determination of a definite order and position for occurrences in time. He does not say whether the occurrences are representations in a subject or states of objects, but in either case to order them in time is to determine whether at some particular point or period in time such occurrences succeed one another in a specific order or are simultaneous with each other. In order to determine this, Kant holds, we have to posit the existence of objects that endure through time – substances – and the existence of determinate patterns of causation and interaction among them. Thus we need to use the fundamental categories of substance, causation, and interaction for time-determination or the "exposition of appearances."

Kant does not explain in any detail *why* we must use these categories to accomplish this end – a fuller explanation of that will await the section of the published *Critique* called the "Analogies of Experience" (A176–218/B218–65). In the *Critique*, the "Analogies" follow a separate argument for the universal and necessary validity of the categories from certain more abstract conceptions of both objects and apperception, which he calls the "Transcendental Deduction of the Pure Concepts of the Understanding" (A84–130 and B116–69). Since in Kant's original sketches of the central argument of his planned *Critique* there is no separation between the discussion of apperception, objects, and the exposition of appearances, and the original discussion of the relation between apperception and objects already has the form of an analogy, it is an enduring question for the interpretation of the *Critique* whether or not the separation of the Transcendental Deduction and the Analogies of Experience have rendered asunder considerations that should have remained joined.

1776–77.   These thoughts seem to be as far as Kant had gotten by 1775. In several further extensive notes from around 1776–77, we find for the first time what looks like an outline for a whole intended book. In the first of these notes, Kant divides his plan under four headings: "Dialectic of Sensibility"; "Dialectic of Understanding – Transcendental Theory of Magnitude"; "Transcendental Theory of Appearance – Reality and Negation"; and "Transcendental Theory of Experience" (R 4756, 17: 698–702). This fourfold division does not, however, imply as elaborate a conception of the intended work as it might seem to, because the first three headings all cover the same ground, namely, Kant's theory of space and time as already stated in the inaugural dissertation. The fourth part adds to this a statement of the three principles of experience involving the concepts of substance, causation, and interaction that were first clearly listed in R 4681. Further, in spite of the fact that the first three sections all have the word "dialectic" in their titles, it is only in the fourth section that Kant explicitly states both theses and antitheses of the kind that we find in the "Dialectic" of the *Critique*, although he also hints at antinomies in the treatment of space and time.

At this point Kant is still experimenting with the organization of his planned work. But the content that he here envisages including is fairly clear: First, about space and time, he maintains that "All space and times are parts of larger ones," and that "All parts of space and time are themselves spaces" and times (R 4756, 17: 701). This implies that there are no simple parts in space and time, that space and time are continuous, and that space and time are infinite yet unitary (no matter how large a region of space or time is, it is always part of *one* larger space or time) (R 4756, 17: 699–701). Kant implies that in order to understand these claims we also have to assume that space and time "are nothing real" (R 4756, 17: 699–700). Under the title of "Dialectic of Understanding – Transcendental Theory of Magnitude" he further states that although the nature of our representation of space and time implies the infinitude of the possible extension or division of space and time, nevertheless "Infinite space and infinite past time are incomprehensible" [*unbegreiflich*] (R 4756, 17: 700). This suggests a conflict between the nature of the intuition of space and time and the nature of an intellectual concept or comprehension of them; but Kant does not explain how this conflict is to be resolved beyond asserting that "Space and time belong only to the appearances and therefore to the world and not beyond the world" (R 4756, 17: 702).

Then Kant turns to the "Transcendental Theory of Experience." Here he asserts three theses:

1. Something as substance, that is matter, neither comes into nor goes out of existence, from nothing comes nothing, i.e., matter is eternal (*ex nihilo nihil in mundo fit*) although dependent.
2. Every condition of the world is a consequence, for in the continuity of alteration everything is starting and stopping, and both have a cause.
3. All appearances together constitute a world and belong to real objects (against idealism). God as a cause does not belong to the world. For only through the agreement of representations with objects do they agree with one another and acquire the unity which perceptions that would be appearances must have. (R 4756, 17: 702)

To the first two theses he opposes what he explicitly labels "antitheses": For (1), the antithesis is that "There is no substance," and for (2), "Then there would be no first cause." Kant is not clear about the source of the conflict between theses and antitheses, although the whole note seems to suggest a conflict between the infinite structure of space and time and the needs of the understanding.

The next note gives a clear picture of the sources of dialectical conflict, while also suggesting that the whole content of the *Critique* could be organized around this conflict. Kant begins by explicitly formulating for the first time a principle that will be crucial in the *Critique*: "The principles of the possibility of experience (of distributive unity) are at the same time the principles of the possibility of the objects of experience." He then suggests that there are two classes of such principles, namely, (1) principles of "Unity of intuition," or principles of "appearance" as such, and (2) the principles of "experiences," or those in accordance with which "the existence of appearances is given." Finally, he suggests how antinomies arise: We get one set of principles from the "empirical use of reason," where the concepts of reason are applied to "space and time as conditions of appearance," and a different set from the "pure use of reason," where space and time are not taken to be conditions of the use of the concepts of reason. On this basis, Kant describes two sets of competing principles that clearly lead directly to the Antinomy of Pure Reason expounded in the *Critique*:

Immanent principles of the empirical use of understanding:

1. There is no bound to the composition and decomposition of appearances.
2. There is no first ground or first beginning.
3. Everything is mutable and variable, thus empirically contingent, since time itself is necessary but nothing is necessarily attached to time.

Transcendent principles of the pure use of understanding:

1. There is a first part, namely the simple as *principium* of composition, and there are limits to all appearances together.
2. There is an absolute spontaneity, transcendental freedom.
3. There is something which is necessary in itself, namely the unity of the highest reality, in which all multiplicity of possibilities can be determined through limits. (R 4757, 17: 703–4)

The first pair of principles from each group stakes out the debate separated into the first two antinomies in the *Critique*, the disputes over whether or not space and time are infinite in extension and over whether or not they are infinitely divisible. The second pair corresponds to the third antinomy in the *Critique*, which debates whether all events have an antecedent cause or whether there is a first cause that has no antecedent cause of its own. The third pair parallels the later fourth antinomy, which debates whether the whole series of events in the world is contingent or has an external ground that is necessary (A426–60/B454–88). However, the conclusion that Kant draws from this presentation of the antinomies is not yet what he will later argue. He clearly suggests that the "transcendent principles" (what will be the theses in the later antinomies) arise from using concepts of the understanding without space and time as conditions, while the "immanent principles" result from applying the concepts of the understanding to space and time and using them within the conditions imposed by the structure of our representations of space and time, using them as "principles of the exposition of appearances." But he does not reject the "transcendent" use of the concepts of the understanding. On the contrary, he still seems to hold, as he did in the inaugural dissertation, that there is a legitimate transcendent use of the concepts of the understanding unrestricted by the conditions of space and time. Thus he reiterates the three subreptic axioms of the dissertation as three "Rules of Dialectic":

1. Do not judge what does not belong to appearances in accordance with rules of appearance, e.g., God with [rules of] space and time.
2. Do not subject what does not belong to outer appearance, e.g., spirit, to its conditions.
3. Do not hold to be impossible what cannot be conceived and represented in intuition, the totality of the infinite or of infinite division.

Then he lists four "principles of the absolute unity of reason" that can apparently be maintained as long as we do not violate any of these three rules:

a. Simplicity of the thinking subject.
b. Freedom as the condition of rational actions.
c. *Ens originarium* as the *substratum* of all connection of one's representations in a whole.
d. Do not confuse the restriction [*Einschränkung*] of the world in accordance with its origin and content with its limitation [*Begrenzung*]. (R 4757, 17: 704–5)

At this point, then, it seems as if Kant envisioned for the *Critique* (1) an account of the nature and structure of space and time paralleling that in the dissertation, (2) a new account of the use of *a priori* concepts of the understanding, according to which they yield "immanent principles for the empirical use of the understanding" only when applied to spatiotemporal representation to achieve an "exposition of appearances," but (3) continued adherence to the view of the dissertation that these concepts can also yield transcendent or metaphysical knowledge when freed of the restriction of the forms of sensibility.

   Perhaps this last point was only a momentary lapse, however, for in the next preserved note Kant says that "The transcendent principles are principles of the subjective unity of cognition through reason, i.e. of the agreement of reason with itself"; "Objective principles are principles of a possible empirical use" (R 4758, 17: 706). This suggests that whatever exactly the use of the transcendent principles of pure reason is, it is *not* to obtain any knowledge of external objects, which can only be achieved through the empirical use of the concepts of understanding, their application to representations in space and time for the exposition of appearances. Kant continues with this thought in the following note, where he lays out four conflicts between "principles of the exposition of appearances," or principles applied to "appearances" for the "unity of experience," on the one hand, and "principles of rationality or comprehension" on the other. These conflicts correspond precisely to the four antinomies of the *Critique*. The first set of principles is:

1. No absolute totality in composition, hence infinite *progressus*,
2. No absolute totality of decomposition, hence nothing absolutely simple,
3. No absolute totality of the series of generation, no unconditioned spontaneity,
4. No absolute necessity.

The opposing set of principles of rationality is:

1. Unconditioned totality of the dependent whole,
2. Unconditioned simple,
3. Unconditioned spontaneity of action,
4. Unconditioned necessary being. (R 4759, 17: 709–10)

Kant says that the latter "propositions are subjectively necessary as principles of the use of reason in the whole of cognition: unity of the whole of the manifold of cognition of the understanding. They are practically necessary with regard to . . . " He does not finish the thought, or explain the practical necessity of the principles of reason. But he is clearly drawing back from the thought that reason by itself furnishes metaphysical cognition of real objects independent of our own thought.

Summing up our results thus far, then, it looks as if by 1777 Kant had come this far in planning the *Critique*. First, it would include the account of space and time as transcendentally ideal pure forms of intuition already reached in 1770. Second, it would include a derivation of three concepts of the understanding – substance, causation, and interaction – and their associated principles as necessary for the exposition of appearances given through the forms of space and time and as objectively valid only in that context. Third, it would include a four-part antinomy pitting those principles, valid for the exposition of appearances, against four opposed transcendent principles, using the concepts of understanding but without restriction by the forms of sensibility, which have no objective validity but can be used in an unspecified way for the unification of empirical knowledge and for some equally unspecified practical purpose. Such a *Critique* would basically have consisted of a theory of sensibility, a theory of experience, and an antinomy of pure reason.

Clearly Kant needed more time to understand the positive function of pure reason, which is only hinted at in these notes. But this is not the only way that the outline of the *Critique* that we can construct for the period around 1777 differs from the work as finally published. There are several other glaring differences.

First, the "transcendental theory of experience," or theory of the "immanent use" of the concepts of understanding, is not yet divided into a transcendental deduction of the categories and a derivation of the principles of judgment used in the exposition of appearances, as it will be in the published work. Second, all of these notes suggest that the content of the "Dialectic" is exhausted by the four antinomies of pure reason, whereas in the published *Critique* the Dialectic is divided into three parts, the "Paralogisms," "Antinomy," and "Ideal of Pure Reason." Can we learn anything about what led to these further divisions of the *Critique* before it finally took on the form Kant gave it in 1779 and 1780?

1778–80. Fortunately, some notes assigned to the period 1776–78 rather than 1775–77 survive and throw light on the final development of Kant's conception of the *Critique*. In one note that has been assigned to the later part of this period, Kant for the first time suggests that there may be a deduction of the categories as necessary conditions of apperception or the unity of consciousness that does not depend upon the temporal character of the data to be unified. Since this may be the earliest surviving sketch of a transcendental deduction conceived of as separate from and antecedent to the argument to the categories as conditions of the possibility of the exposition of appearances, or what Kant would come to call the "Analogies of Experience," it is worth quoting this passage in full:

> In everything passive or what is given, apprehension must not merely be found, but it must also be necessitated in order to represent it as given, i.e., the individual apprehension must be determined by the universal. The universal is the relation to the others and to the whole of the state. By being distinguished from the arbitrary is it considered as given, and only by being subsumed under the categories is it considered as something. It must therefore be represented in accordance with a rule by which appearance becomes experience and by which the mind comprehends it as one of its actions of **self-consciousness,** within which, as in space and time, all *data* are to be encountered. The unity of the mind is the condition of thinking, and the subordination of every particular under the universal is the condition of the possibility of associating a given representation with others through an action. Even if the rule is not immediately obvious, nevertheless one must represent the object as amenable to a rule in order to conceive it as that which represents something, i.e., something which has a determinate position and function among the other determinations. (R 5203, 18: 116–17)

This note, which is very similar to a crucial passage in the version of the "Transcendental Deduction" published in the first edition of the *Critique* (A108), is notable for two reasons.

On the one hand, it clearly suggests that there must be general rules for the unity of consciousness that can be characterized independently of specific rules for time-determination, although the way remains open for a further inference that once the temporal character of the data for consciousness is considered, then these general rules may give rise to further rules which are themselves temporal in content. Such a separation between the most general form of rules for the unity of consciousness and the specific rules for the unity of a consciousness that is temporal in character, along with the necessity of explaining the relation between the two forms of rules, will be central to the organization of the *Critique of Pure Reason*. Here Kant will offer, first, a transcendental deduction of the pure concepts of the understanding as conditions of the possibility of any unity of consciousness in general, under the rubric of an "Analytic of Concepts"; second, a derivation from those general rules of more specific rules for time-determination, under the rubric of a "Schematism of the Pure Concepts of the Understanding" (A137–47/ B176–87), which is in turn part of, third, the "Analytic of Principles," in which Kant argues for specific principles involving the temporally interpreted categories, such as the principles of the conservation of substance and of universal causation, as necessary conditions of objective time-determination. The introduction of the concept of schematism, which Kant first records in a note from 1778–79 with the statement that "We must subject all of our pure concepts of the understanding to a schema, a way of putting the manifold together in space and time"(R 5552, 18: 220), is required precisely by the explicit separation of the transcendental deduction of the categories from the analogies by means of which Kant had previously derived the categories.

On the other hand, this note also reveals a fundamental ambivalence about exactly *how* the categories are to be derived from the general idea of the "unity of consciousness," an ambiguity continuing one already found in the materials from 1775. In one strategy, rules are necessary to distinguish an arbitrary series of representations from the orderly or rule-governed series of representations by means of which a determinate *object* is presented to consciousness; on this account, the "unity of consciousness" would mean the unity of consciousness characteristic of the presentation of an object. Alternatively, Kant suggests that rules are necessary for the unity of consciousness as a form of *self-consciousness*, the recognition that various representations, whatever objects they may or may not represent, all have the unity of belonging to a single *mind*. Kant does not clearly separate these two strategies, nor suggest a means for connecting them. This ambiguity will plague all of Kant's attempts to find a definitive form for the deduction of the categories. It runs throughout the first-edition version of the "Deduction," and then leads Kant to continue to experiment with the proper form for the deduction, not merely in the second edition of the *Critique*, in which he completely rewrites the "Deduction," but in the intervening period, in which he tries to resolve the ambiguity in the *Prolegomena to Any Future Metaphysics* (§§14–23, P 4: 294–306), the *Metaphysical Foundations of Natural Science* (introduction, MFNS 4: 474–6 n), and a number of surviving drafts (especially R 5923, 18: 385–6; and R 5930–4, 18: 390–3), and on into the 1790s as well, where he continued to tinker with the deduction in his drafts for an essay on the *Real Progress of Metaphysics from the Time of Leibniz and Wolff* (PM 20: 271–7). Arriving at a definitive interpretation of the transcendental deduction of the categories has been one of the most challenging tasks for Kant scholarship, and this underlying ambivalence in Kant's conception of its strategy is a large part of the reason for this problem.

Kant never resolved the issue of the fundamental strategy of the deduction of the categories, but much else about the content and structure of the *Critique* had clearly been resolved by 1778–79. Several extensive drafts from this period show that Kant had not only arrived at the final organization of the "Transcendental Analytic," but also that he had now arrived at the final organization of the "Transcendental Dialectic," which is also more complicated than the schemes he had been considering in the period 1775–77. Whereas in the notes from that period Kant presented the material of the "Dialectic" as a single set of antinomies, now he has divided the material into three main parts, the diagnosis of "three kinds of transcendental illusion" generated by "three kinds of rational inference" (R 5553, 18: 223). Thus, at this point Kant envisioned the following argument:The constructive argument of the book would consist of two main parts. The first of these would in turn be broken into two further parts. The first would be the account of space and time that had been in place since 1770; in the *Critique* Kant would finally entitle this the "Transcendental Aesthetic." Then in the second part, under the title of "Transcendental Analytic" that he now introduces (R 5553, 18: 221), Kant would make the argument, based on the principle that "We can have synthetic cognition *a priori* about objects of experience, if [it] consists of principles of the possibility of experience" (R 5552, 18: 220), that would link a transcendental deduction of the categories to a demonstration of their role in empirical time-determination by means of an intervening schematism of those categories. This argument, showing that the categories must be applied to representations given in space and time in order to yield unity of consciousness and objective experience of objects, would have the consequence that by concepts "we cognize only objects of the senses," thus that the categories "do not reach to the supersensible."

It would then be the burden of the second main part of the work, which Kant had already been referring to as a "Dialectic" for several years, to show that "Even though the concepts [of the pure understanding] extend to all objects of thought in general," "they do not yield any amplification of theoretical cognition," but may nevertheless have a "practical-dogmatic" role in a "practical regard, where freedom is the condition of their use" (R 5552, 18: 220). Now Kant divides this critical part of the work into three divisions. He argues that it is characteristic of pure reason to assume as a "petition" or "postulate" the principle that "All conditioned cognition not only stands under conditions, but finally under one which is itself unconditioned," or that "If the conditioned is given, then the entire series of all its conditions is also given" (R 5553, 18: 222–3; in the *Critique*, see A307–8/B364). He now argues that because there are three kinds of rational inference, from a property to its subject, from a property to another property, and from a property to its ground, there must be three dialectical inferences back to an unconditioned or absolute substance, an unconditioned or absolute whole, and an unconditioned or absolute ground. Thus reason postulates "the unconditioned subjective conditions of thinking, the unconditioned (objective) condition of appearances, and the unconditioned objective condition of all things in general" (R 5553, 18: 226). These three inferences, which Kant will discuss in the *Critique* under the titles of the "Paralogisms," the "Antinomy," and the "Ideal of Pure Reason," will be diagnosed as theoretically unjustified, because the underlying principle, that whenever the conditioned is given so is its ultimate condition, is theoretically unjustified. Nevertheless these three ideas of the unconditioned will be useful in a practical context.

Even in the *Critique* Kant will retain the argument that the three forms of "transcendental illusion" arise from three forms of inference (e.g., A306/B363), but he also suggests both in these notes and in the published work that they arise directly from an unwarranted reification of the three concepts of a subject, a series, and a ground (A323/B380), and it is easier to understand his diagnosis in these terms. Thus, the three fundamental errors of metaphysics are the assumptions (1) that because we assign all of our thoughts to ourselves as subjects, we have knowledge of the soul as an absolute subject; (2) that because we place all appearances in series of ever-increasing spaces and times, of ever-decreasing spaces and times, of causes and effects, and of contingents necessarily dependent upon something else, we have knowledge of completed extensions in space and time, of simples in space and time, of a first cause, and of a necessary ground for all contingents; and (3) that because we must think of some ground for any possibility, we have knowledge of an absolute ground of all possibilities. In Kant's words:

> The idea of the soul is grounded on [the idea that] the understanding must relate all thoughts and inner perceptions to the self and assume this as the only permanent subject.
>
> The idea of the unconditioned for all conditions in appearance is grounded in reason as the prescription to seek the completeness of all cognition of the understanding in [series of] subordination.

> The idea of the unconditioned unity of all objects of thought in an *ens entium* is necessary in order to seek the relationship among all possible [things] ... (R 5553, 18: 226)

Kant suggests that it is natural for us to form these ideas, and that there is even a subjective necessity to do so, but that it is a mistake to interpret them as offering theoretical knowledge of objects of a kind that could never be presented by the senses.

What led Kant to divide his diagnosis of metaphysical illusions concerning the self, the world, and God into these three parts – rational psychology, rational cosmology, and rational theology – when previously the claims about the soul were simply instances of the second and third antinomies (the simplicity of the soul was just an instance of simplicity in general, and the freedom of the self just an instance of absolute spontaneity), and an absolutely necessary ground of all contingents was the subject of the fourth antinomy (R 4747, 17: 705)? The contents of the third part of the "Dialectic" in the published *Critique*, the "Ideal of Pure Reason," suggest that Kant elevated the discussion of rational theology into a separate section simply because he had too much material to treat it as a single antinomy – he recapitulates his critique of the ontological, cosmological, and physicotheological arguments from the *Only Possible Basis* of 1763 as well as criticizing his own positive argument from that work, even while retaining the arguments about God that constitute the third and fourth antinomies in the *Critique*. Kant would also have been hard put to integrate his positive account of the necessary rational genesis of an ideal of pure reason ("Transcendental Dialectic," book II, chapter III, section 2; A571–83/B599–611) into any discussion that took the form of an antinomy.

The criticism of rational psychology in the "Paralogism," however, is something new, which appears in these notes of 1778–79 for the first time. Here one can conjecture that the new section is Kant's response to his own new transcendental deduction of the categories: Because he has claimed that the *unity of consciousness* is an *a priori* necessity from which we can deduce the validity of the categories, he now also has to tell us to be careful what *not* to infer from this unity of consciousness, namely any metaphysical claims about the *soul*, claims that the *subject* or *bearer* of consciousness is a unitary, simple, and eternal substance. Such a "paralogism of pure reason" would really be "a transcendental subreption," an illusion in which "the unity of apperception, which is subjective, would be taken for the unity of the subject as a thing" (R 5553, 18: 224–5). We find no such warning in Kant before we find the introduction of a separate transcendental deduction of the categories from the unity of consciousness; so we can assume that the expansion of the

"Dialectic" to include paralogisms of pure reason separate from the second and third antinomies was Kant's own warning about what not to read into his deduction.

One last note, written on a matriculation record from March 1780, adds a reference to one final section of the forthcoming *Critique*:

To the *Canon*: the end of the whole of metaphysics is God and the future and the end of these [in] our conduct, not as though morality must be arranged in accordance with these, but because without these morality would be without consequences. (R 5637, 18: 273)

This is cryptic, and can be fully understood only in light of the argument that Kant develops, over all three *Critiques*, that the highest good or maximization of both virtue and happiness can only be conceived of as being made possible by an intelligent and benevolent author of the world prepared to give us the time necessary to perfect our virtue and to make the world suitable for the achievement of our ends. In the Canon, hope for the happiness of which we have made ourselves worthy belongs to the motivation for virtuous action and is presupposed by its rationality. It is only after 1785 that Kant treats the moral incentive as distinct from the hope for deserved happiness and sufficient for moral motivation. But assent to the conditions of the possibility of the highest good will remain a requirement of practical reason. And this ground of moral belief or faith is the practical use to which Kant will put the theoretical illusions of metaphysics. Conceiving of a "canon" of pure reason as well as its critique – that is, a doctrine of its positive practical use as well as the negative criticism of its misguided theoretical use – was thus the final stage in conceiving of the structure and content of the *Critique*, where this "canon" would be expanded into a "Doctrine of Method" that would accompany the "Doctrine of Elements," into which the "Transcendental Aesthetic," "Transcendental Analytic," and "Transcendental Dialectic" would be placed.

With all of this in place by 1780, Kant was finally able to write the *Critique*, and to announce to Herz on May 1, 1781, after a decade of apologies and postponements, that "In the current Easter book fair there will appear a book of mine, entitled *Critique of Pure Reason*" (Corr 10: 266–7). Ten days later, he wrote these lines to Herz:

My work, may it stand or fall, cannot help but bring about a complete change of thinking in this part of human knowledge [metaphysics], a part of knowledge that concerns us so earnestly. For my part I have nowhere sought to create mirages or to advance specious arguments in order to patch up my system; I have rather let years pass by, in order that I might get to a finished insight that would satisfy me completely and at which I have in fact arrived; so that I now find nothing I want to change in the main theory (something I could never say of any of my previous writings), though here and there little additions and clarifications would be desirable. (Corr 10: 268–70)

5 Kant's Defense and Revision of the *Critique*

Kant never intended the *Critique of Pure Reason* to be more than a propaedeutic to the systematic metaphysics of nature and of morals that he had long intended to write. He proceeded shortly to the first part of this system, publishing the *Metaphysical Foundations of Natural Science* in 1786, in which he tried to show that the application of his general principles of judgment to the empirical concept of motion yields the basic principles of Newtonian physics, and took the first step toward the second part with the *Groundwork for the Metaphysics of Morals* in 1785, intended as the introduction to the detailed system of duties that would constitute the metaphysics of morals. The latter would not however appear until 1797. But the initial reception of the *Critique of Pure Reason* sorely disappointed Kant's expectation that the work could not "help but bring about a complete change of thinking," and a great deal of Kant's effort during the decade of the 1780s was devoted to the unforeseen task of clarifying the critical foundations of his system of philosophy that he thought he had completed in May 1781. This work took a number of different forms: the publication of a brief defense and attempted popularization of the *Critique* in 1783, the *Prolegomena to Any Future Metaphysics*; continued work on the transcendental deduction in his private notes during 1783–84; a proposed revision of the transcendental deduction of the categories in the introduction to the 1786 *Metaphysical Foundations of Natural Science*; a substantial revision of the *Critique of Pure Reason* for its second edition in 1787; and finally the publication of two further critiques, the *Critique of Practical Reason* (1788) and the *Critique of the Power of Judgment* (1790), which were clearly not works Kant had planned at the time of the publication of the *Critique of Pure Reason* but which instead grew out of his ongoing struggle to clarify the foundations of his critical philosophy (as well as to address some previously unaddressed topics, such as the nature of taste and art and of biological science, all in the third *Critique*). We cannot comment on all this material here; instead, after some brief comments on the revisions to the *Critique of Pure Reason* that are implicit in the *Prolegomena* and *Metaphysical Foundations of Natural Science*, we will conclude this introduction by outlining the main changes made in the second edition of the first *Critique*.

The first serious review of the *Critique* was published in the *Göttingischen Anzeigen von gelehrten Sachen* for 1782. The university at Göttingen, which had been founded in 1737 by George I of England in his continuing capacity as Elector of Hanover, was home to a group of empiricist philosophers led by J. G. H. Feder (1740–1821). The review, abridged and rewritten by Feder from a much more sympathetic draft by the Berlin moral philosopher Christian Garve (1742–98), was in spirit highly dismissive. The version of the review published by Feder omitted Garve's careful, sympathetic exposition of much of Kant's arguments and his quite insightful interpretation of Kant's justification of the possibility of synthetic *a priori* cognition in general, and in mathematics in particular, to focus on three objections.[9] First, it charged that Kant's "system of the higher or … transcendental idealism" was nothing but a restatement of Berkeley's idealism, reducing all objects to our own sensations and leaving the real existence of any objects beyond our own representations entirely unknown. Second, it argued that on Kant's account there could be no differentiation "between the actual and the imagined, the merely possible … mere visions and fantasies." Third, it charged that Kant's argument that the unsound theoretical use of pure reason can and must be replaced by a sound practical use was entirely unnecessary, since morality already has a sound foundation in common sense.

Kant had apparently already formulated the intention to write a popular presentation of his critical philosophy almost as soon as the *Critique* was published, but the hostile review clearly galvanized him, and he included explicit answers to some of its charges in the *Prolegomena to Any Future Metaphysics* that he published in August 1783. Specifically, he differentiated his position from Berkeley's idealism by maintaining that he denied the real existence of *space* and *time* and the *spatiotemporal properties* of objects, but not the real *existence* of objects themselves distinct from our representations. For this reason he proposed renaming his transcendental idealism with the more informative name of "formal" or "critical idealism," making it clear that his idealism concerned the *form* but not the existence of external objects (P 4: 288–93). Further, he argued that his theory of the understanding and its principles, unlike the usual brands of idealism, offered determinate principles for establishing the coherence of veridical experience as contrasted to incoherent dreams and fantasies (P 4: 290–1), and that for this reason it should not be considered a form of "higher" idealism, an expression in which he detected a pejorative implication of fancifulness, but rather a philosophy firmly rooted in the "fruitful **bathos** of experience" (P 4: 373 n). Finally, Kant rejected any

---

9. For translations of both versions of the review, see Brigitte Sassen, Kant's Early Critics: The Empricist Critique of the Theoretical Philosophy (Cambridge: Cambridge University Press, 2000), pp. 53–77. Garve subsequently shared his original draft with Kant, and they remained cordial correspondents.

comparison of his view to Berkeley's on the ground that Berkeley's empiricism leaves all knowledge of space and time *a posteriori* and contingent, whereas only Kant's own formal idealism can explain our *a priori* knowledge of space and time as the universal and necessary forms of intuition (P 4: 287–8, 374–5).

Emphasizing that only his transcendental idealism can explain our *a priori* knowledge of mathematics and pure physics while at the same time demonstrating that as formal idealism it is entirely compatible with the real existence of external objects would both be major objectives in Kant's revisions of the *Critique* for its second edition. Vindicating his view that the illusory theoretical use of pure reason must be replaced by its sound practical use, the last point challenged by the Göttingen review, although not replied to in the *Prolegomena*, would also be an aim of those revisions. But, as with his earlier response to the criticism of his inaugural dissertation, Kant also revealed in the *Prolegomena* a concern that his critics had not raised: namely, a concern about the adequacy of the transcendental deduction of the categories itself. Kant expressed this worry about the deduction (and the associated paralogisms) as mildly as he could: He says that he is completely satisfied with the "content, order, and doctrine" of his work but that he is "not entirely satisfied with the presentation in some parts of the Doctrine of Elements, e.g., the deduction of the categories or the paralogisms of pure reason" (P 4: 381). In fact, Kant would rewrite both of those chapters for the second edition of the *Critique*, in part to respond to the challenge to his variety of idealism raised by the Göttingen review but also to respond to his own concerns about their persuasiveness.

Indeed, Kant had already begun to manifest his concern about the adequacy of the deduction in the *Prolegomena* itself. Following what he claims to be the "analytic" method of the *Prolegomena* rather than the "synthetic" method of the *Critique* (P 4: 263–4), Kant replaces the transcendental deduction of the categories, which purports to analyze the necessary conditions of the possibility of the transcendental unity of apperception, with an analysis of the necessary condition of universally and necessarily valid judgments in mathematics and natural science, the conditions of which are then supposed to be the conditions of the possibility of experience in general. This method of argument makes no use of the concept of apperception at all. Kant argues that while mere "judgments of perception," which make no claim to necessary objective validity or the agreement of others, but only report how things seem to a single subject, use the logical forms of judgment, "judgments of experience," which do make claims to objective validity necessary for all, can only derive their universal and necessary validity from their use of *a priori* categories to make the otherwise indeterminate use of the forms of judgment determinate (P 4: 297–302). Kant pursues this approach even further in the preface to the

Metaphysical Foundations of Natural Science, three years later, where he suggests that the categories can be derived as the necessary conditions of making the use of the logical forms of judgment determinate without explicit reference to the alleged distinction between judgments of perception and of experience (MFNS 4: 475 n). But although this strategy avoids the obscurity of some of Kant's claims about the transcendental unity of apperception, it is open to the charge of begging the question against both empiricists and skeptics by proving that the categories are necessary only by presupposing an interpretation of ordinary and scientific knowledge-claims as universally and necessarily true that neither a skeptic nor an empiricist would dream of accepting.

In any case, Kant's notes from 1783–84 show that he continued to experiment with both the unity of apperception as well as the concept of objectively valid judgment as possible bases for the deduction of the categories (see especially R 5637, 18: 271–6; R 5643, 18: 282–4; R 5923, 18: 385–7; and R 5929–34, 18: 389–94). However, when Kant came to rewrite the chapter on the transcendental deduction for the second edition, he returned to his original strategy of trying to combine the conditions of possibility of the unity of apperception with those of the judgment of objects to create an unshakable foundation for the objective validity of the categories.

When Kant was first notified by his publisher in April 1786 that a new edition of the *Critique* would be needed, he apparently contemplated a drastic revision that would include an extensive discussion of practical reason as well as a restatement of his work on theoretical reason. At the same time, however, he also assumed the rectorship of his university. At some point during the year he must have decided on the more modest though still extensive revisions that we have, which incorporate none of the developments in Kant's moral philosophy we find in the *Groundwork* of 1785. Enough of these revisions were completed by January 1787 for typesetting of the new edition to begin, and all of the revisions were apparently completed by that April, just a year after the new edition was first requested. The main changes in the second edition, growing partly out of Kant's response to the criticism of the first edition and partly out of his own concerns, as we have just described, may be summarized as follows.

(1)   Kant replaced the preface to the first edition, which speaks in only the most general terms about the need to place the science of metaphysics on a secure footing, with a considerably longer one that describes in much more detail both the innovations of Kant's critical method – it is here that Kant introduces the famous comparison between his own anthropocentric procedure in philosophy and Copernicus's heliocentric revolution in astronomy (Bxvi) – and his position

that pure reason ultimately has a positive role only in its practical rather than theoretical use (Bxxiv–xxxvii). The latter emphasis is clearly meant to respond to the dismissive remarks of the Göttingen review on this subject. The new preface concludes with a brief comment on the changes in the new edition, and then with a long footnote (Bxxix–xli) revising yet further the new "Refutation of Idealism" that is one of the most important of those changes.

(2)   The introduction is considerably expanded. Its main changes are, first, a more detailed discussion of the distinction between *a priori* and *a posteriori* cognition than the first edition had included, and then an extended argument that the synthetic *a priori* cognitions of pure mathematics and physics can only be explained by transcendental idealism, which are in fact lifted virtually without change from the *Prolegomena* (B14–19; see P 4: 267–9). Kant's inclusion of these pages shows that he was still very concerned to emphasize the difference between Berkeley's idealism and his own, since Berkeley's inability to explain *a priori* knowledge was one of Kant's chief charges in the *Prolegomena*.

(3)   The "Transcendental Aesthetic" is also considerably expanded. Kant's aim here seems to have been primarily to buttress the (anti-Berkeleyan) argument for the necessity of his transcendental idealism to explain synthetic *a priori* cognition, rather than the argument that his form of idealism is compatible with knowledge of the real existence of external objects, which will dominate his revisions in later parts of the work. Thus, Kant divides his previously undivided discussions of space and time into what he now calls the "Metaphysical" and "Transcendental Exposition" of each, where the first of these titles subsumes the arguments that space and time are pure and *a priori* forms of intuition as well as pure intuitions in their own right, and the second separately expounds the argument that our synthetic *a priori* cognition of mathematics (especially geometry) can only be explained by transcendental idealism. The revised version of the "Aesthetic" concludes with a number of additional arguments in behalf of transcendental idealism that were not present in the first edition (B66–73).

(4)   The next major change comes in the "Transcendental Deduction" of the categories: Two introductory sections are left largely unchanged, but the third, containing the actual argument, is completely rewritten. In spite of his experiments with an apperception-free deduction in 1783 and 1786, Kant now tried to ground the entire deduction more clearly on the starting point of the unity of apperception than he had in 1781. At the same time, trying to salvage his experiments of the intervening years, he also tried to connect the unity of apperception more unequivocally with the idea of the objective validity of judgment than he had in the earlier version. Second, Kant tried to prepare the

way for the coming new "Refutation of Idealism" by stressing that the cognitive subject must be regarded as determining the structure and order of its own self-consciousness just as much as it does the representation of external objects (§§23–5). Finally, continuing the stress on the necessity of the representation of space that was part of the *Prolegomena*'s response to the charge of Berkeleyan idealism, Kant now emphasizes that the synthetic unity of consciousness is responsible for the unity of both space and time, and indeed that the representation of determinate *spatial* relations is a necessary condition for the representation of a determinate *temporal* order, which is an undeniable feature of any conceivable self-consciousness (see B156).

(5)   The argument that while time is the form of all sense, the representation of space is itself the necessary condition for the representation of determinate order in time, which continues Kant's rebuttal of the charge of Berkeleyan idealism, is the chief theme of all of the revisions in the "Analytic of Principles." These revisions take the form of restatements of the several principles of judgment, and of additional paragraphs at the start of each of the proofs; but Kant's most important addition to this part of the book is the new "Refutation of Idealism" that is inserted into the discussion of actuality in the "Postulates of Empirical Thought" (B274–9). This may seem like an inauspicious location for such an addition, but Kant's intention in choosing it can only have been to show that empirically meaningful judgments about the modalities of possibility and necessity all depend upon connection to the actual in perception, and then to show what he means by the actual in perception: that which we judge to exist independently of our representation of it, even if we also know that the *form* in which we represent the independence of such objects is itself dependent upon the constitution of our own sensibility. The "Refutation of Idealism," in other words, is Kant's ultimate attempt to prove that his idealism is *merely* formal idealism rather than the metaphysical subjectivism of Berkeley.

The "Refutation of Idealism" is one of the most important of Kant's additions to the second edition, but the fact that before the new edition was even published he was already revising this revision in the new preface shows that Kant was hardly satisfied with his new argument. In fact, the new "Refutation" is not so much the culmination of a long-considered process of thought as the beginning of a new one, and a dozen or more further versions surviving from 1788–90 show that Kant continued to work on this argument even after the second edition of the *Critique* had already appeared (R 5653–4, 18: 206–13; R 5709, 18: 332; R 6311–17, 18: 607–29; and R 6323, 18: 643–4).

(6)   Kant also undertook major revisions in the chapter on the distinction between phenomena and noumena. His primary concern in these revisions

was to clarify the difference between using the concept of a noumenon in a negative and a positive sense. This can be regarded as a step toward clarifying his doctrine that whereas pure reason has only a negative theoretical use it does have a positive practical use, a doctrine the clarity of which had been challenged both by the Göttingen review and also by Garve's original draft.

(7)   Having added the new "Refutation of Idealism," Kant had no choice but to rewrite at least the fourth paralogism of the first edition, a passage that had clearly provoked the charge that Kant had just repackaged Berkeleyan idealism by insisting that we could be as certain of the objects of outer sense as of those of inner sense because objects in space are nothing but one species of representation alongside representations of inner sense (see especially A370). Kant replaced this argument with an anti-Cartesian argument that there should be no puzzle about the possibility of interaction between mind and body, one of the central philosophical issues of Kant's youth, because the differences in their appearances that Descartes and his followers had assumed to stand in the way of interaction might be no more than different appearances of a single, unknown kind of underlying reality (B427–8). However, Kant did not confine himself to this change, but took the opportunity to rewrite and simplify the whole chapter on the paralogisms. Except for his substantive change in the fourth paralogism, this is the only part of his revisions that lives up to his pretense of merely improving his manner of exposition (Bxxxvii).

Beyond the "Paralogisms of Pure Reason," Kant made no further significant changes for the second edition. His continuing restatement and refinement of many important doctrines touched upon in the remainder of the book, such as his further work on freedom of the will and the postulates of practical reason in the second *Critique* and on the regulative use of the ideas of reason in the third, suggest that rather than remaining content with the remainder of the first *Critique*, Kant came to realize how much work remained to be done. The richness of all his writings of the late 1780s and 1790s are testimony to this awareness.

Bibliography

The literature on the *Critique of Pure Reason* and Kant's philosophy as a whole is vast. The following works, all in English except for the standard German edition of Kant's works and a recent German edition of the *Critique*, are just an introduction.

Texts

Kant, Immanuel. *Kant's gesammelte Schriften*. Edited by the Royal Prussian, subsequently German, then Berlin-Brandenburg Academy of Sciences. 29 vols. Berlin: Georg Reimer, subsequently Walter de Gruyter & Co., 1900—. (*Akademie* edition)

Kant, Immanuel. *Kritik der reinen Vernunft*. Edited by Jens Timmermann. Hamburg: Felix Meiner Verlag, 1998.

Volumes from The Cambridge Edition of the Works of Immanuel Kant, edited by Paul Guyer and Allen W. Wood

Kant, Immanuel. *Opus Postumum*. Edited and translated by Eckart Förster and Michael Rosen. Cambridge: Cambridge University Press, 1992.

Kant, Immanuel. *Theoretical Philosophy 1755–1770*. Edited by David Walford in collaboration with Ralf Meerbote. Cambridge: Cambridge University Press, 1992.

Kant, Immanuel. *Critique of Pure Reason*. Edited and translated by Paul Guyer and Allen W. Wood. Cambridge: Cambridge University Press, 1998.

Kant, Immanuel. *Correspondence*. Edited and translated by Arnulf Zweig. Cambridge: Cambridge University Press, 1999.

Kant, Immanuel. *Theoretical Philosophy after 1781*. Edited by Henry E.Allison and Peter Heath. Cambridge: Cambridge University Press, 2002.

Kant, Immanuel. *Notes and Fragments*. Edited by Paul Guyer, translated by Curtis Bowman, Paul Guyer, and Frederick Rauscher. Cambridge: Cambridge University Press, 2005.

Surveys of Kant's Philosophy

Guyer, Paul. *Kant*. Second edition. London: Routledge, 2014.

Walker, Ralph C. S. *Kant*. London: Routledge, 1978.

Ward, Andrew. *Kant: The Three Critiques*. Cambridge: Polity, 2006.

Wood, Allen W. *Kant*. Oxford: Blackwell, 2005.

Biography and Background

Beck, Lewis White. *Early German Philosophy: Kant and His Predecessors*. Cambridge, MA: Harvard University Press, 1969.

Kuehn, Manfred. *Kant: A Biography*. Cambridge: Cambridge University Press, 2001.

Schönfeld, Martin. *The Philosophy of the Young Kant: The Precritical Project*. New York: Oxford University Press, 2000.

Watkins, Eric, ed. *Kant's Critique of Pure Reason: Background Source Materials*. Cambridge: Cambridge University Press, 2009.

Essay Collections

Altman, Matthew C., ed. *The Palgrave Kant Handbook*. London: Palgrave Macmillan, 2017.

Bird, Graham, ed. *A Companion to Kant*. Oxford: Blackwell, 2006.

Guyer, Paul, ed. *The Cambridge Companion to Kant*. Cambridge: Cambridge University Press, 1992.

Guyer, Paul, ed. *The Cambridge Companion to Kant and Modern Philosophy*. Cambridge: Cambridge University Press, 2006.

Guyer, Paul, ed. *The Cambridge Companion to Kant's Critique of Pure Reason*. Cambridge: Cambridge University Press, 2010.

Kitcher, Patricia, ed. *Kant's Critique of Pure Reason: Critical Essays*. Lanham: Rowman & Littlefield, 1998.

O'Shea, James R., ed. *Kant's Critique of Pure Reason: A Critical Guide*. Cambridge: Cambridge University Press, 2017.

Commentaries and Monographs

Abacı, Uygar. *Kant's Revolutionary Theory of Modality*. Oxford: Oxford University Press, 2019.

Allison, Henry E. *Kant's Transcendental Idealism: An Interpretation and Defense*. Second edition. New Haven, CT and London: Yale University Press, 2004.

Allison, Henry E. *Kant's Transcendental Deduction: An Analytical-Historical Commentary*. Oxford: Oxford University Press, 2015.

Ameriks, Karl. *Kant's Theory of Mind*. New edition. Oxford: Oxford University Press, 2000.

Anderson, R. Lanier. *The Poverty of Conceptual Truth: Kant's Analytic/Synthetic Distinction and the Limits of Metaphysics*. Oxford: Oxford University Press, 2015.

Bennett, Jonathan F. *Kant's Analytic*. Cambridge: Cambridge University Press, 1966.

Bennett, Jonathan F. *Kant's Dialectic*. Cambridge: Cambridge University Press, 1974.

Bird, Graham. *The Revolutionary Kant: A Commentary on the Critique of Pure Reason*. LaSalle, IL: Open Court, 2006.

Buroker, Jill Vance. *Kant's Critique of Pure Reason: An Introduction*. Cambridge: Cambridge University Press, 2006.

Dicker, Georges. *Kant's Theory of Knowledge: An Analytical Introduction*. New York: Oxford University Press, 2004.

Friedman, Michael. *Kant and the Exact Sciences*. Cambridge, MA: Harvard University Press, 1992.

Gardner, Sebastian. *Kant and the Critique of Pure Reason*. London: Routledge, 1999.

Grier, Michelle. *Kant's Doctrine of Transcendental Illusion*. Cambridge: Cambridge University Press, 2001.

Guyer, Paul. *Kant and the Claims of Knowledge*. Cambridge: Cambridge University Press, 1987.

Guyer, Paul. *Reason and Experience in Mendelssohn and Kant*. Oxford: Oxford University Press, 2020.

Höffe, Otfried. *Kant's Critique of Pure Reason: The Foundation of Modern Philosophy*. Dordrecht: Springer, 2010.

Kemp Smith, Norman. *A Commentary to Kant's Critique of Pure Reason*. Second edition. London: Macmillan, 1923.

Kitcher, Patricia. *Kant's Transcendental Psychology*. New York: Oxford University Press, 1990.

Kitcher, Patricia. *Kant's Thinker*. New York: Oxford University Press, 2012.

Longuenesse, Béatrice. *Kant and the Capacity to Judge: Sensibility and Discursivity in the Transcendental Analytic of the Critique of Pure Reason*. Translated by Charles T. Wolfe. Princeton, NJ: Princeton University Press, 1998.

Melnick, Arthur. *Kant's Analogies of Experience*. Chicago: University of Chicago Press, 1973.

O'Shea, James R. *Kant's Critique of Pure Reason: An Introduction and Interpretation*. Durham: Acumen Publishing, 2012.

Paton, Herbert James. *Kant's Metaphysic of Experience*. 2 vols. London: George Allen & Unwin, 1936.

Strawson, Peter F. *The Bounds of Sense: An Essay on Kant's Critique of Pure Reason*. London: Methuen, 1966.

Tonelli, Giorgio. *Kant's Critique of Pure Reason within the Tradition of Modern Logic*. Hildesheim: Georg Olms, 1994.

Van Cleve, James. *Problems from Kant*. New York: Oxford University Press, 1999.

Watkins, Eric. *Kant and the Metaphysics of Causality*. Cambridge: Cambridge University Press, 2005.

Weldon, T. D. *Kant's Critique of Pure Reason*. Second edition. Oxford: Clarendon Press, 1958.

Willaschek, Marcus. *Kant on the Sources of Metaphysics: The Dialectic of Pure Reason*. Cambridge: Cambridge University Press, 2018.

Wolff, Robert Paul. *Kant's Theory of Mental Activity: A Commentary on the Transcendental Analytic of the Critique of Pure Reason*. Cambridge, MA: Harvard University Press, 1963.

Cambridge Elements ≡

The Philosophy of Immanuel Kant

Desmond Hogan
Princeton University

Desmond Hogan joined the philosophy department at Princeton in 2004. His interests include Kant, Leibniz and German rationalism, early modern philosophy, and questions about causation and freedom. Recent work includes 'Kant on Foreknowledge of Contingent Truths,' *Res Philosophica* 91 (1) (2014); 'Kant's Theory of Divine and Secondary Causation', in Brandon Look (ed.) *Leibniz and Kant*, Oxford University Press (forthcoming); 'Kant and the Character of Mathematical Inference', in *Kant's Philosophy of Mathematics Vol. I*, Carl Posy and Ofra Rechter (eds.), Cambridge University Press (2020).

Howard Williams
University of Cardiff

Howard Williams was appointed Honorary Distinguished Professor at the Department of Politics and International Relations, University of Cardiff in 2014. He is also Emeritus Professor in Political Theory at the Department of International Politics, Aberystwyth University, a member of the Coleg Cymraeg Cenedlaethol (Welsh-language national college) and a Fellow of the Learned Society of Wales. He is the author of *Marx* (1980); *Kant's Political Philosophy* (1983); *Concepts of Ideology* (1988); *International Relations in Political Theory* (1992); *Hegel, Heraclitus and Marx's Dialectic; International Relations and the Limits of Political Theory* (1996); *Kant's Critique of Hobbes: Sovereignty and Cosmopolitanism* (2003), *Kant and the End of War* (2012) and is currently editor of the journal *Kantian Review*. He is writing a book on the Kantian Legacy in Political Philosophy for a new series edited by Paul Guyer.

Allen Wood
Indiana University

Allen Wood is Ward W. and Priscilla B. Woods Professor emeritus at Stanford University. He was a John S. Guggenheim Fellow at the Free University in Berlin, a national Endowment for the Humanities Fellow at the University of Bonn and Isaiah Berlin Visiting Professor at the University of Oxford. He is on the editorial board of eight philosophy journals, five book series and the Stanford Encyclopedia of Philosophy. Along with Paul Guyer, Professor Wood is co-editor of the Cambridge Edition of the Works of Immanuel Kant and translator of the *Critique of Pure Reason*. He is the author or editor of a number of other works, mainly on Kant, Hegel and Karl Marx. His most recently published books are *Fichte's Ethical Thought*, (Oxford University Press, 2016) and *Kant and Religion* (Cambridge University Press, 2020). Wood is a member of the American Academy of Arts and Sciences.

About the Series

This Cambridge Elements series provides an extensive overview of Kant's philosophy and its impact upon philosophy and philosophers. Distinguished Kant specialists provide an up to date summary of the results of current research in their fields and give their own take on what they believe are the most significant debates influencing research, drawing original conclusions.

Cambridge Elements ≡

The Philosophy of Immanuel Kant

Elements in the Series

A full series listing is available at: www.cambridge.org/EPIK

CPSIA information can be obtained
at www.ICGtesting.com
Printed in the USA
LVHW081609050821
694404LV00019B/1008